DIRECTING FITNESS

Redefining the Fitness Director Role for the Training Studio

BY

Zachary J. Columbia

DIRECTING FITNESS

Copyright © 2020 by Zachary J. Columbia.

All rights reserved. No part of this publication may be reproduced, distributed, or transmitted in any form or by any means, including photocopying, recording, or other electronic or mechanical methods, without the prior written permission of the author, except in the case of brief quotations embodied
 in critical reviews and certain other non-commercial uses permitted by copyright law.

Ordering Information: Quantity sales. Special discounts are available on quantity purchases by corporations, associations, and others. Orders by U.S. trade bookstores and wholesalers.

DREAMSTARTERS

www.DreamStartersPublishing.com

ZACHARY J. COLUMBIA

Table of Contents

Introduction 4

Why I Really Became a Trainer 10

Life In 50 Minutes 17

What Is a Fitness Director? 29

Your Gym, Your Church 43

Retention 101 61

If You Build It, They Will Stay 80

Systemization & Optimization 110

The Medical Assistant Close 142

Success Stories Only 159

Redefining The Fitness Director 165

Directing Fitness Coaching Program 175

Introduction

Being a personal trainer is like mission impossible. No, not the action-packed movie with ridiculous stunts. It's truly, a real mission impossible. Anyone pursuing a career in fitness quickly realizes the path to success is not smoothly paved or paved at all for that matter. The complexities of the fitness industry, the psyche of the client-coach relationship, and the overwhelming consumption of every ounce of energy a trainer has to give, is absolutely daunting.

Training is totally the wrong term for what we do anyway. You coach a person; you train a dog. If you want to have success in this industry, then you must be a coach and an exceptional one at that. Unfortunately, that's not all though. Today's personal "training" client requires way more than professional program design and form instruction. Quite frankly, they require a level of perfection in every aspect of business, customer service, and consistency that is – well -- impossible. That's not to say that you can't get close, but there are thousands of gym owners out there struggling to bring it all together, and probably a million trainers who are absolutely clueless.

Did you know trainers last less than a year in the industry? Fact! It's hard, bro! Not the training obviously; if all we had to do was train peeps, it would be the all-time greatest job in the world. "Pull this!" "Press that!" "Squeeze your shoulders," "Back flat!" Discouragingly, there is a whole lot more that goes into getting and keeping training clients that incoming personal trainers don't understand, but quickly learn once on the job.

If you have your own gym, oh man, you know the pressure is on. We're talking high stakes, like "putting your house up for collateral" serious. You must attract the clients, sell the clients, onboard the clients, train the clients, and keep the clients. You wish it were that easy. I forgot to mention that you also have to train a staff, clean the gym, answer the phone, address client issues, clean the gym, and build a unique gym culture... wait. What about accounting and finance, cleaning the gym, business operations, dealing with staff issues, cleaning the gym, repairing equipment, keeping up on trends, and networking? And oh... did I mention cleaning the gym?

If you're a gym owner, you know exactly what I'm talking about. If you're an employee of a gym, a director, or a trainer, then maybe you know what I'm talking about, but most likely you don't really grasp what it fully encompasses. Success in this industry requires a deep understanding of the investment and sacrifice that was made, and exactly what's at stake if the business fails. A deep understanding from the entire team, not just the owner, is a necessary perspective. Taking it on as a nearly impossible challenge is the only way it can be fun, and really the only way anyone can persevere through it.

Sometimes I wonder how I ever hung on as long as I did in the industry before I came to this realization. Honestly, it wasn't from lack of trying to do something else. That passion for fitness though! Am I right? I'm sure if you're reading this book, then you know what I'm talking about. Seriously, working in the fitness industry seemed like such a good idea at one time. I mean after all, it's what we are all passionate about, right? Of course, it's easy to lose that passion once you realize how difficult it is to get others to see the importance of it and prioritize it in their own lives. It's easy to go running for the door as soon as you realize what success in this industry requires.

I've been a personal trainer, then an operations manager for a construction company, then a personal trainer again, and then a regional sales manager for a marketing company. Like they say, the third time's the charm! The learning curve was/still is steep, but when giving up is no longer an option, that's when you become unstoppable.

When I decided once and for all that this was it, that the fitness industry was the only career path for me, my view started to change. I began to recognize the big picture of what

I was actually doing. I started to understand the business side of the industry and within a short-time, I went from fitness coach to fitness director at one of the most successful training gyms nationwide. Have there been tough days? Like every single one! Has it been fun? Absolutely!

I decided to write this book when I was jaded. Jaded on a personal level from wanting so badly to turn my passion for fitness into a successful career, but struggling to pay my bills. Jaded on a professional level from having a career that has no prestige and is often looked down on. And Jaded from pouring all my energy into training clients who would inevitably give up and quit. I told myself that I was going to figure it all out and when I had, I would write a book about the struggle. I'll admit -- this didn't exactly end up being the book I envisioned writing.

You see, when I became the director at Pulse, I started to see things from a mile-high view looking down. I truly began to understand why success in the fitness industry is so incredibly difficult, especially for the training studio. It seems like the ones that have thrived are few and far between. You might find this surprising if you scroll Instagram and see all the ads of trainers telling you how easy it is, while they sit on an exotic sports car. Anyone in the trenches can see straight through their B.S. Anyway, I digress. What I realized is the undeniable need for a structured, high-performing team being led and given direction by what I believe to be the most crucial role in the business. When I sat down and started writing, I wondered if anyone out there had ever brought it together and presented it the way I intend to do in this book. There are none, at least that I know of, that share with you how to have a proper director role or how to efficiently and successfully direct a gym; that's exactly what this book sets out to do.

These stories and strategies are not just for the fitness director or the gym owner alone, but for the personal trainer and support staff members of a team who need to understand the remarkable complexities of the fitness industry.

As fitness director, my role is to connect trainer to gym owner and bridge the gap between fitness and business. In this book, my goal is to outline the roles and different perspectives of clients, trainers, and gym owners, and how to bring those all together. In doing so, we understand what the fitness director role is, and why it's so important to the success of the training studio.

This book speaks both to the gym owner and the director. For the gym owner, it explains why you need the role, what responsibilities the director should have, how to manage the position, and gives you a literal instruction book that you can hand them and say, "Read this and do it!" For the director, this book is your guide. It's your instruction manual. It includes lessons and best practices that I've learned from directing one of the most operationally-sound training gyms you'll find anywhere in the world. This is Directing Fitness.

Chapter 1

Why I Really Became a Trainer

My wife is hot!

I'm not bragging. That's really why I became a trainer. Here's the story:

Before I became a trainer, I was just your average gym patron. I would walk in, punch in my phone number, scan my finger, and head to the locker room. After putting my things in the locker, I would murder, and I mean absolutely murder the weights. Haha, just kidding. Seriously though! I loved everything about the gym and something about the environment just resonated with me.

One day I walked into the gym just like every other day, but this time, standing behind some bald front desk guy was hands-down the most beautiful woman I had ever seen in my life. When I had finished checking in, she looked at me, smiled, and said, "Have a nice workout Zach." Now, I don't want to get too hopelessly romantic here or anything, but I knew. I just knew. There was a voice in my head telling me that she was the woman I was going to marry.

Pretty much all I did for that whole workout and every workout for the next year, was think about her the entire time. Every time she happened to be working at the front desk, I would check-in, we'd chat a little, but nothing more than that. I'll admit it, I didn't have much game! I mean really though, how many guys do you think hit on the most beautiful woman on the planet in just one work shift? There was no way I was coming off as a gym creep.

Finally, one day, fate stepped in. While I was ravenously destroying the weights on a chest and tri day, the Fitness Manager walked up to me and interrupted my workout by asking if I had ever thought about being a trainer. He totally charmed me, saying that he had been watching me and that I "really knew my stuff." Looking back, this guy was desperate for some trainers, and I guess I was the poor schmuck who took him up on his offer.

DIRECTING FITNESS

Really, I only took the job because I was in love with the girl at the front desk and thought this might finally be my chance. Now, I knew at the time that it seemed a little crazy, so I didn't want to invest too much. Instead of legitimately looking for a credible certification course, I took the most inexpensive route possible. I found an outdated NASM book at the library of the community college I was attending. Honestly, it was the only time I ever set foot in a library during my college years, but that's beside the point.

The book seemed fairly good, but there was no way I was going to take the NASM exam – it was way too expensive. Instead, I studied that book harder than anything else I had ever studied for in my life. After one month, I went online, paid for an ACE exam, and scheduled my test date. Now, I don't know about you, but I don't really believe that studying for an exam with the wrong book is the best idea. Regardless, I passed the test by a very slim margin. Long story short, I had my certification, took the job, and I've been married to that super hot front desk girl ever since. I know, I know... hopelessly romantic.

So, what does my story teach us about running a fitness business?

First, the standards to become a personal trainer are obviously terrible. Second, well, keep reading...

You see, just like when I saw my wife-to-be for the very first time, fitness enthusiasts fall in love with the idea of becoming a trainer. They believe they've found their passion, their one true love, and that they're going to live happily ever after with it as their career. I'm here to tell you that love at first sight is dangerous in this industry. (This is why there's so much turnover.) Sure, in my case it may have worked out, but do you think it really was as simple as "long story short?" Of course not! Just like falling in love is pretty easy, there is always that "Oh" moment where you realize it's not all rainbows and unicorns. A career in the fitness industry is no different. Love for fitness might get you started in the industry, but the honeymoon is short-lived. Any experienced trainer knows it doesn't take long before that "Oh" moment, and directors experience that moment almost every single day.

We live in a world today where loyalty is not common. People jump from relationship to relationship, from brand to brand, or from career to career. If you have this mindset, you'll become another fitness industry statistic. Another gym owner closing their doors or another trainer lasting less than a year in the fitness industry.

Here is what I believe to be the most important point I make in this book. If you remember nothing else, remember this: IF YOU WANT TO BE SUCCESSFUL IN THE FITNESS INDUSTRY, YOU HAVE TO MARRY IT!

I'm not talking "marry it" like today's marriage statistics. I'm talking understanding the sanctity of marriage as it was intended. You do it once! You look behind you and burn all other bridges so to speak. You have to eliminate all other possibilities. Quite frankly, it's just way too flipping hard and only the truest of coaches survive.

For most reading this book, it's too late for you. You didn't realize that personal training was like that amazing girl you met at the one bar that one night. Yep... you "knocked up" the fitness industry and now you're tied to it.

Want success? Want happiness? Want recognition, money, and the joy that comes from helping others? Marry it and see what happens! Eliminate all other possibilities. See what happens to your ability to build loyalty with your clients (which is like being married to each one of them, by the way). See what happens to your ability to sell memberships. See what happens to your ability to lead and inspire a staff, to build a gym culture, to extend your influence outside the confines of your gym walls and into the community and industry as a whole. Marry it!

Redefine and Reconnect

What made you want to become a trainer?

_____
_____
_____
_____
_____
_____
_____
_____

What makes you continue to be a trainer?

_____
_____
_____
_____
_____
_____
_____
_____

"Action is the foundational key to all success."

Pablo Picasso

Chapter 2

Life In 50 Minutes

A Day in The Life

I've always said that if I were to write a book about being a personal trainer, I would call it "Life In 50 Minutes." Trainers live their lives in 50-minute increments. They start training at 5:00am, finish training at 5:50am, run to the bathroom, grab a bite to eat and some caffeine, check Instagram, and prep for the next client(s), all in the span of 10 minutes. Then, they start over again at 6:00am (if they have enough clients).

The different personalities, interactions, and excuses can all be pretty entertaining and often very comical. It's definitely a unique career with its own set of challenges.

DIRECTING FITNESS

While standing there telling people what to do all day may not seem like that taxing of a job, it absolutely is. If it's done the way it should be done, if the coach is coaching, engaged, and leading the workout, then it can be exhausting. Add in the personal interaction that takes place between a client and a coach, and it becomes both physically and mentally draining.

Just imagine having to adapt to the differences in personalities. Imagine the countless conversations that take place every day. Imagine keeping track of everyone's program, and everyone's goals. Then on a deep personal level, learning about their husband/wife, their children, their boss and coworkers, and their childhood, all while correcting form and providing motivation.

As a trainer you have to be ready for literally anything! From a client confiding in you about a rocky relationship with their spouse, to their Dr. Jekyll & Mr. Hyde attitude. If your business uses a semi-private training model that allows trainers to work with multiple clients at one time, then you can multiply all of this by four, five, or even six. Spend a few hours coordinating that many clients, and having that many conversations, and your head will be swimming.

Imagine pausing a conversation, to go have another conversation with a client while correcting their form, then running to a different client to explain their next block of exercises. This is all while keeping an eye out on everyone else to make sure they're performing each movement correctly, while remembering where you left off with the previous two conversations. You then return to the first client and jump right back into the conversation but have to be brief. You do this because you don't want any of the other four clients you're simultaneously training, to feel like they're not getting enough of your attention! It's really just controlled chaos, but it's a dance, it's a performance, and being good at it is an art.

We Get No Love

As a Fitness Coach, I was asked frequently by my clients what I wanted to do professionally. It was implied that what I was doing wasn't my career choice. The question always saddened me, and I thought, "What do you mean, what do I want to do?"

For years, the fitness industry screwed itself with poor standards and shady sales tactics. Personal trainers have a bad rap and rightly so. When most people think of personal trainers, they think of a young college kid who has the physique of a Greek god or goddess, but who is probably just working their way through school before they move on to a "real career." To be fair, that was me when I first started out, especially the physique part... The difference was that I cared enough about my client's success to continue learning. There are several differences between personal trainers and fitness coaches, but that's the main one. Fitness Coaches are career-oriented professionals who care! They didn't get their certification over a three-day weekend in a conference room at a Holiday Inn Express. A Fitness coach is a highly trained and highly educated expert with vast amounts of knowledge on the human body, exercise, nutrition, and psychology. Not to mention, being a coach is their career. (Gym owners and directors: never hire personal trainers. Instead, hire true, career-oriented coaches!)

Nursing is a highly respected career. To become a Registered Nurse, you must receive a college education in the field of Nursing and then take the National Council Licensure Examination. After becoming an RN, nurses must renew their license every few years, depending on state requirements.

A reputable, career-oriented fitness coach goes through the same level of education and examination as a nurse, though these two career paths are viewed so differently. Nursing is looked at as a prestigious career, personal training isn't.

If you're wanting to have a successful training gym, then this can't be the case. Coaches should have Bachelor and/or Master's Degrees. They should have completed internships with professional sports teams or top training facilities. They should be Manual Therapists, Nutrition Coaches, Corrective Exercise Specialists, Golf or TPI Specialists, Flexibility Specialists, etc. They should be treated and viewed as knowledgeable professionals!

 Give your coaches the respect they deserve and use your gym to set the standard for what a coach should be. I'm not just ranting. I bring it up because being successful in this industry requires knowledge and experience. It requires energy and vibrance, it requires professionalism and tact, and it requires communication and performance. Coaches live their lives in 50 minute performances. From the second they walk out onto the training floor; they must be performing for the client. Sure, they must be an expert, but they also must be a performer. The reason there is a whole chapter devoted to this topic is because the success of a training gym rides and dies on the coaches. They're the reason the clients will keep coming back, day in and day out. If they aren't a true coach, if they aren't walking on stage and performing every hour of their shift, then the business will suffer. Keep that in the back of your mind.

Trainer Brain

Taking multiple clients through a great workout while conversing with each one individually and delivering exceptional customer service that creates a positive experience for each and every member, every single day, every hour of the day for eight hours straight, is an artform. It's not impossible, it just takes a special individual to be able to accomplish this day in and day out. Ask yourself, how long would you be able to keep this up before burning out?

Think, about it -- is there any other customer service-based business out there where you see and interact with the same clients almost every single day? I don't even want to see my best friends every day! It's very difficult for a business to deliver the exact same experience every hour of every day for every member over and over again. However, to be successful in the fitness industry, consistency of the experience is a requirement.

Investing time and energy into others and seeing their success is unbelievably rewarding in the trainer brain. It's literally the reason why coaches get into the industry. Conversely, continually seeing clients fail and/or quit can destroy a coach's morale and cause burnout. It can be extremely easy for a coach to lose sight of the big picture.

When a coach loses sight of the big picture, you lose the coach!

A hard pill to swallow in the fitness industry is the fact that results are not what determine success. As a new director, I made the mistake of putting too much emphasis on results and pressuring my team to get our clients results. While results are a nice side-effect, they're not the main reason customers will continue to come to your gym. The idea of results gets the customer to walk through the front door, but the perceived value is what keeps them coming back day after day.

When a coach invests in members' success, but the members continue to fail, they lose sight of the big picture. We all know having clients focus only on results will destroy their morale and it's no different with your coaches. Performance should not be gaged solely on the client's results. The reality is that you cannot force results on every single member; after all, they're only under your control a few hours a week. You can, however, force them to have a great experience every time they enter your facility. The experience is what gives the members the perception of value. Emphasize this to your team. Make it crystal clear that a member who doesn't visit the gym frequently is going to have no perceived value because they're not experiencing it. Focus your team's performance on first, getting members into the gym, and second, on delivering an amazing experience for your members. Putting this kind of emphasis on the experience instead of just the results, will keep both the coach and the client from getting discouraged. Additionally, it will keep the coach focused on the big picture.

They're Not the Same

As director, your ability to thrive in this industry requires you to understand three particularly important things, two of them we just discussed:

You need to get in the coach's brain. As a director or gym owner, it can be easy to forget the day-to-day grind that trainers go through. Putting yourself in their shoes and understanding that the structure of their day can impact how effective you are at managing the team.

You need to get in the member's brain. Put yourself in their shoes and understand the member experience – specifically understand their interaction each time they visit the facility for a workout.

You need to take these two perspectives and manage directly to them through the systems outlined in this book.

The member brain and the coach brain don't always match up. Think about this. If you're the director or gym owner, you have a mission to accomplish. You met with each and every client before they became a member. You know what their goals and expectations are because you set them. You understand the member brain, but does your team? More importantly, can your team live up to those expectations based on the training you've provided them and the systems you have in place to help them perform? Coming from the perspective of the member, you need members to be held accountable so that they show up, you need them to have a great experience, and they need to see results.

To accomplish this, you need your team behind you. Naturally, your expectation is for the team to not only deliver a great workout, but to also develop relationships with the members and hold them accountable. Additionally, your team needs to get great results, ask for referrals, regularly spread a specific message or make an announcement, and perform on certain metrics. These include being timely, greeting each member with a smile, educating the clients, monitoring the level and appropriate energy of the music, saying "please" and "thank you," and stopping to introduce themselves to anyone doing a tour at the gym. What's more? This is all done in 50 minutes!

The reality is that none of this is a reality without the proper training and development of the team. This also requires support systems in place that enable them to perform in all of these areas. Thankfully, the deeper and deeper you get into this book, the more you will understand how to connect the member brain and coach brain to make meeting these expectations a reality.

Redefine and Reconnect

How can you be more devoted and connected to your clients, while also being able to take in more?

_____
_____
_____
_____
_____
_____
_____
_____

How can you better your team?

_____
_____
_____
_____
_____
_____
_____

"Don't follow the crowd, let the crowd follow you."

Margaret Thatcher

Chapter 3

What Is a Fitness Director?

Time Suck of Training

Okay, here's the deal -- most gym owners get their start as a personal trainer at some box gym. Then, they break off on their own and become a self-employed independent trainer. After running a successful "training business" for several years, they decide to open their own gym. However, they don't start acting as the business owner. Instead, they remain self-employed. Sure, they might own a gym and even have a few employees working for them, but they're not functioning like a business owner. Being self-employed means if you don't show up to work, the work doesn't get done. Being a business owner means being able to step away and the business keeps running.

As anyone reading this book probably already knows, running a gym is not easy. It requires a lot of grunt work, as well as a lot of meticulous attention to detail. New gym owners typically find themselves overwhelmed with training clients, marketing, nurturing leads, performing sales consultations, cleaning the gym, hiring, and training staff. And that's really just the beginning, because there is a whole other side to running a gym, including: supply inventory, maintenance, HR and payroll, licensing, leasing, taxes and finance, etc. Not only is it too much for one person, but it becomes a vicious cycle. Let me explain.

It's not uncommon for new gym owners to find themselves starting their day at 4am, training four or five hours, then following up with leads, then training another four or five hours, then meeting with prospective clients. They do this only to find out that those prospective clients can only train at a specific time that isn't already available, meaning they'll have to devote another hour of the day to training. They need the money though, and want to continue to grow the business, so they sign them up and promise them those time slots anyway! SOUND FAMILIAR? When gym owners find themselves in this situation, working 80 hours a week to keep the business running and never taking a day off or seeing their family, they do one of two things -- they either try to offload the training, or they close down!

It's a natural transition for a new gym owner to quickly recognize the time-suck of training. This is especially true when they're the only one capable of doing everything else a gym requires. Although it sounds like an obvious solution, dropping training off their list of responsibilities doesn't provide the freedom they want. Those hours that were once devoted to training rapidly get filled with managing staff, programming workouts, and performing more consultations. Again, the gym owner recognizes that this is a total misallocation of resources and that their time would be better spent driving the business forward. Naturally, they decide the business needs a fitness director who will manage the other trainers, create the programming, and maybe even perform consultations and sales.

What I just described to you is almost always the natural progression in the training biz and it's exactly why I decided to write this book! If this is you or you're a fitness director and were given this book by your boss, then I can give myself a little pat on the back knowing that I reached my target reader.

Fitness Director?

If you're a gym owner, it's important to ask yourself, "What do I want from my business?" and "What do I want for my life?"

What do I mean? Like I already mentioned, if the business owner steps away, the business keeps running. In the business model I just described, the owner can't step away from the business, even if they have a fitness director! Having a fitness director is great and all, but there is so, so, so, much more to running a successful gym than just training. As an owner, you may have offloaded training, you may have offloaded programming and sales, and managing the training staff, but did you end up with all this free time? Of course not! You may be in a better position to drive the business forward, to focus on building a better community and a stronger gym culture, but you're still tied to the business by the hip.

This is why we need to redefine the fitness director role to a position that allows the gym owner to step away from the business and know everything is going to be well... business as usual.

What is a fitness director? Well, I think the title fitness director is kind of misleading. I've worked in big box gyms that have fitness directors or fitness managers. Their role is micro-focused on managing just the training staff and training sales.

Big box gyms also have a general manager or gym director. I would compare this role more closely to what you should have even in a training studio. I refer to the gym owner and director almost interchangeably. They're not really the same, but as I already explained, the gym owner typically starts off as the director before mentoring someone else to take over. Sometimes the gym owner never hires a director, which is perfectly fine, as long as that's the lifestyle they want.

Regardless, of whether you are a gym owner or director, I'm going to teach you how to successfully run the day-to-day operations of a training business in the remainder of this book.

Understand that the director role is a combination of day-to-day manager of operations, team leader, business analyst, and high-level strategist. Managing the day-to-day of a gym is comprehensive, but the second there is a lull, the mindset must shift. That time is both critical and precious and should be used for analyzing data and strategizing. They should function as the point man or face of the business and oversee just about every aspect of the business except the few areas the owner wants to keep for themselves. They should be vested in the business and treat it as their own, allowing the owner to pursue other business ventures or avenues.

DIRECTING FITNESS

Let me share a short story with you about my transition into the role of fitness director at Pulse. I took over as director probably at the worst possible time for Tim, the owner. He was traveling pretty much non-stop during the first couple of months of me being in my new role. For most business owners, this would have been a terrifying scenario, but I thought it was great. I relished in the opportunity to be able to take over, handle the day-to-day and have him return to a gym that was crushing it. I tried to be in as little contact with him as possible. I knew he was busy and honestly, I didn't want him involved. Not because I was fearful, but because I was confident that I could handle it and I wanted to prove it. When things popped up that I wasn't sure how to do or respond, I simply asked myself, what would I do if I were the owner and this was my business? When things finally settled down and Tim was back in town, we had more members than when he left, and the gym hadn't burned down. I think we both considered it a win, even though we weren't really crushing it yet.

I know this situation would not be the norm in most cases. What I do know, is that taking ownership, continually improving, and being a leader are all necessary qualities of a director. A fitness director must be capable of wearing many hats, and while I'll show you how and why to implement many systems, policies, and procedures in the coming chapters of this book, it's important to keep in mind that the role of director is unique. It's unique in the sense that it's not about just directing the team, but also the clients, and sometimes the owner. The director needs a strong business acumen, but also must be an exceptionally good mediator.

While writing this book, I was racking my brain searching for a way to sum up who a Fitness Director really is and what they really do. I thought about all that I do, from a business standpoint, from an interpersonal relationship-building standpoint, and from a leadership standpoint.

There were few concepts I felt that painted a clear and precise picture as comparing the role to that of a politician.

Just as coaches are performers, directors are politicians. They live in the public eye, so to speak. As a leader, they must interact, build relationships with, and most importantly, listen to all the members and the staff. Their decisions will be scrutinized constantly and they will be held personally responsible for the decisions they make and the quality of the client experience.

One particularly important role of the director is to represent the clients, just as a politician represents their voters. This requires getting in front of the members, understanding how they interact with the business, what drives them, what they need and want from the staff, and gives the director -- wait for it -- A SENSE OF DIRECTION!

Director/Direction

Director/Direction do you get it? I mean do you really get it!? Let's go full circle, literally, so you fully grasp every important element of the role.

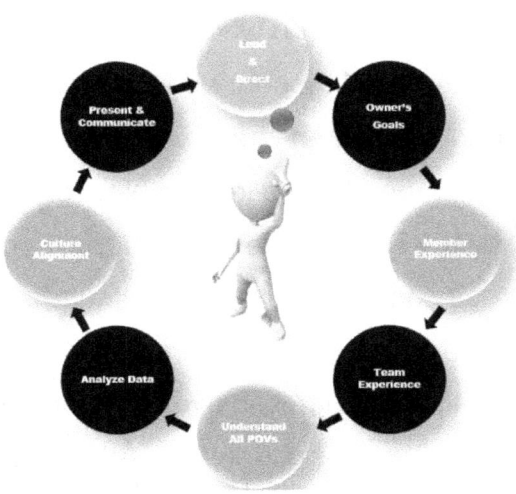

The above diagram is really a never-ending cycle of the decision-making process and the role of the director. Of course, understanding the owner's goals for the business and viewpoint is critical. Sometimes it may be the director acting alone with the owner's goals in mind, or it may be the owner communicating a specific idea to the director. Oftentimes though, the gym owner isn't interacting as closely with the members or the team day in and day out. That's why they have the director in the first place. Therefore, it's important for the director to understand all viewpoints and take into account how decisions will impact each party.

The director should be closely in tune with the members and the team. He or she should understand what the members want and should be able to use this viewpoint in the decision-making process. Likewise, the director should also understand the team's perspective and how the team will respond to certain decisions.

The next step is to analyze the data. What do the numbers say? How will a decision impact the bottom line? Once the director has a clear understanding of how a decision will impact both the members and the numbers, it's their duty to present and argue both to the owner. Obviously, if you can't find an angle that will benefit the business financially, there isn't really any point. Unfortunately, the right decision usually doesn't stand out, mostly because it's impossible to please everyone. It's not uncommon in these situations to be stuck between wanting to add to the bottom line and pleasing the members or team. Those are the tough ones, and fortunately while it's the director's job to argue each side, it's not usually the director's job to make the final decision. Once the owner makes the final call, however, the director must leap into action.

This is where direction comes in. The director shouldn't have to be told how to execute. He or she should understand how to create a plan, establish support from both the team and the members, and provide direction and leadership to get the job done. Essentially, the director must go out and muster up support from the members and staff. Creating buy-in isn't always easy; it requires trust, confidence and a great deal of charisma. You can see why it's necessary to wear many hats and why it can be a very political position.

Characteristics

Additionally, the director role requires a certain level of emotional maturity few seem to possess. This is really what should be defined as "professionalism." I love having fun at work, I mean after all, it is a gym. I like to joke around with my team and with the members. I like to laugh and poke fun at everyone's mistakes or unique attributes. I love it even more when the members and team give it right back to me. I think being able to laugh and have fun, and then turn around and get right down to business is important in any work environment.

With that being said, I've been frustrated and driven to a point of being infuriated by prospects, members, and my staff. Did they know it? Did they see my frustration? Never! The director requires a level of maturity to handle any situation with composure, tact, and a well-thought-out response.

Along with emotional maturity, a level of fortitude and perseverance is an absolute must. Most days, I fight (not literally) with at least one member. I don't look at it as fighting with them; rather, I fight for them over staying or leaving. Sometimes I win, sometimes I lose.

It can be discouraging when someone falls off and loses focus of why they joined in the first place. It's important for the director to never let anything stop them, or even slow them down for that matter. The director needs to put their head down and go. Win or lose, never stop fighting, never even slow down.

Again, this is why it's so important to be married to the fitness industry.

What I'm really saying is that it's about the client. They trust us with their health and invest in us. Unfortunately, most "professionals" in the fitness industry make it about themselves and their own fitness. Show me a coach who posts pictures of their client's successes on social media instead of themselves shirtless, and I'll show you a true coach. Directors understand that it's not about them.

Another point I'd like to make here, is that I don't believe it's necessary to be feared. I believe being loved is nice, but most importantly, I believe in being respected.

Respect is something that must be earned, and necessary to have if you want to be an effective leader. I can confidently say that I'm well-respected by the owners of Pulse. I have the love and respect by every member of my team, and of course, the respect of the members as being the expert who follows through.

Finally, the director is the captain of the team. Their role is to take a bunch of individual employees and turn them into a cohesive team with a universal goal and unified systematic approach. Easier said than done, especially in the fitness industry where trainers commonly think of themselves as independent, but a team approach is what winning requires here.

Redefine and Reconnect

What do you want for your business?

_____
_____
_____
_____
_____
_____
_____

Now, how can The Director help you accomplish that?

_____
_____
_____
_____
_____
_____
_____

"A true leader has the confidence to stand alone, the courage to make tough decisions, and the compassion to listen to the needs of others. He does not set out to be a leader, but becomes one by the equality of his actions and the integrity of his intent."

Douglas MacArthur

Chapter 4

Your Gym, Your Church

Go to Church

In 2018 I developed thoracic outlet. A rare syndrome, thoracic outlet occurs when the clavicle and first rib compress around the brachial branch, cutting off blood flow to and from the arm. Although rare, it's common among baseball players and I've spent a great deal of my life on a baseball field. Due to lack of blood flow, I developed severe clotting, had a pulmonary embolism, seven surgeries, and along with a couple cool looking scars, earned myself a lot of debt.

DIRECTING FITNESS

Towards the end of the whole ordeal, the owner of Pulse, along with some of the members set up a Go Fund Me page and Pulse hosted a charity Thanksgiving Day boot camp with me as the beneficiary. The turnout and generosity of the members were absolutely overwhelming to say the least. In recap, I told my team that this type of thing doesn't normally happen in a business; it's more of the type of thing you'd expect from a church.

I'm going to stop right here. If you're considering working in the fitness industry and you've never been to church, do yourself a favor -- go, experience it, observe it, and learn from it.

I mean no offense here, but a great number of people feel obligated to go to church. Many would rather be watching football and drinking beer than listening to a sermon, but they go anyway. They chat and socialize, they sit and listen to the sermon, they pray, and then they leave feeling surprisingly good about going. To some, the socializing and sense of community doesn't matter, they go for the sermon, for the message. They're devout. On the other hand, some want both. In my experience, most go because they feel obligated, and stay because of the sense of community and having a support system.

The gym is no different!

What percentage of your members would rather be tailgating and drinking beer instead of working out? Most don't necessarily love working out, but they feel obligated to go. They feel like it's something they are supposed to do.

A lot of your members aren't coming for the sermon, but they'll stay for the good feeling they get from being a member. What most members need is a sense of community, socialization, support, and a great feeling of accomplishment. Some may just come for the workout; they are your true believers. Some want both. Most however, need to be reminded daily of why working out is important so that they feel obligated to keep going.

Churches pack their auditoriums every weekend with a combination of people all there for different reasons. You know what they do well? They appeal to each one. They keep people feeling obligated to go and they promote a unique sense of community and support that only their members have access to. They socialize, they hold events, they unite behind different charity causes, and they continue to show up every week, week after week. Learn from them -- build your church!

DIRECTING FITNESS

Your Gym, Your Culture

Owning or managing a fitness business is all-consuming, and I've heard a lot of horror stories. Honestly, it's something I've struggled with over the years. It's definitely a challenge to train clients, lead a team, market and sell, manage the finances and operations, and all the other millions of tasks that go with it. None of these responsibilities factor in anything personal you might also have going on.

So many out there are working 80+ hours a week just to keep their doors open. It's not just the workload or the stress of it all, but also the consumption of your soul by the demands of the clients. It can affect your home life, your relationships, and your health if you let it.

It's funny, we love our clients so much. They become our friends and confidants, but we can never take a day off. Scratch that -- we can never take a minute off! If you work in the fitness industry, then your main job is not being a fitness professional. You are first and foremost a performer, a rock star. Rock stars are rock stars 24/7/365. They live it! They never take a minute off because it's inherently who they are as a person! Even when they're not face-to-face, they're projecting it on social media.

Fitness is no different... you know, except for the money and lavish lifestyle. Really though, trainers have fan clubs. How often do you tell someone what you do, and they immediately ask you how to lose weight or get rid of the fat on their arms? It can be exhausting sometimes to be performing every minute of the day. Add in all the other stresses that go with running a business -- any business – and it can be very easy to forget why you wanted a career in this industry in the first place. Subsequently, what ends up happening is you lose your culture.

It's easier said than done when you have a hundred million things to do and you're trying to keep it all together, but you have to remember your culture. Your culture is your brand and it's hands down, the most important thing your gym has. It's the one thing that differentiates someone doing a squat in your gym, vs. doing a squat somewhere else. It's what gives the member a sense of belonging and ownership and earns their loyalty.

Your culture is really your X factor. It's what communicates to the prospective member that the reason they've never been successful in the past is because they've never been a member of your gym before. We all have an idea of what we want our gym's culture to be, but really knowing it and keep it is extremely difficult

One of the main reasons gyms lose their culture is because we try to be everything to everyone. Gym owners be like: "Athletes, yeah we train them." "Geriatrics, yep."

"Bodybuilders, duh." "Middle-aged men trying to get their mojo back, no doubt." "Desperate housewives, of course." "You want splits? Yeah we do splits." "You're looking for functional training, we do that too." "Oh, power lifts, "I can teach you how to do power lifts."

In planning to open their business, gym owners think their target market is going to be a little more specific. Then when they get into the business, the realization sets in that they just need clients! This is an especially important lesson for the director who is focused on sales and growth. While it's totally fine to be accommodating up to a certain point, you can't sacrifice your gym's culture for one person. You may gain a short-term client, but you'll lose your identity. Ultimately, you want members to be invested in your success and the way you get there is by members buying into your culture.

So the question remains, how can you continue to be the leader of your fitness business's culture when all your time is gone, you're drained from the clients, you're stressed over getting clients, and you're trying to accommodate everyone? You say "No!"

First, you must learn to say no. I'll be perfectly honest, I'm a "yes man." Always have been. If someone asks me to do something or needs help, I say "yes," even if I don't want to. It's just who I am inherently, and I've always wanted to please people. Always saying "yes" can be a huge detriment in this industry, though. It took me a long time to learn to say "no" to clients and prospective clients. It's something that I still struggle with, but what I've come to understand is that always saying "yes" hurts the business in the long run.

Second, you cannot create a healthy gym culture if you don't have a clear understanding of who you are and what you do. We'll get more into numbers later, because that's really the foundation you build off of, but unless you're running a charity training studio, maximizing profits should be your main priority. Once you understand your model and how your business makes its money, you can develop your culture around that model. The easiest way to start is actually the hardest…

You have to say "no" to anything and anyone that doesn't align with your culture, even if they're an existing customer that gives you money every month. That's definitely not an easy thing to do -- actually it's the hardest thing to do! You don't have to flip a switch, though. You can work toward it in phases.

Understand this, the fastest way to get where you want the business to be is straight there. Every time you say "yes" to something that doesn't align with the direction that you're headed in, it becomes a time suck and a roadblock. As director, I've learned this too well. I began to understand this when I looked at all the problems, complaints, and cancellations I was dealing with, that were taking up so much of my time. I realized that 90% of the issues were coming from the lowest paying members who we were accommodating but didn't really fit in with the direction the gym was headed.

Most start off in the fitness industry as rock stars, but instead of living it 24/7/365, they end of losing their passion and start faking it. I truly believe that having the fitness career you always wanted is as easy as saying "no." Gym owners need to sit down with their directors, take a hard look at the numbers, and then determine their culture, their brand, and their identity.

Once you know it, own it. Interweave it so tightly into your offering that you have no other choice than to stick to it and say no to anything that doesn't align with it.

A Sense Of Community

Community and culture really go hand in hand when it comes to training gyms. I must give a major shout out here to Tim and Erin Lyons, owners of Pulse Fitness. When I first started working at Pulse Fitness, I was blown away by the warmth and closeness of the members. While the members were great people to begin with, the community of the gym was really harnessed and brought out by the efforts of both

Tim and Erin. I've never seen two business owners work harder or focus more on community. What's more astounding is that they created a business model that allowed them to work in the background promoting a strong client-focused community through their team, instead of having to interact face to face with the members daily.

Something that I think they recognized early on, is that as a gym, your community is without question the most powerful retention tool you will ever have. The community almost eliminates the concern for results and accountability. Almost! When your gym gives members a place of belonging, a place where they develop friendships, a support system, and the enthusiasm to grow that community, your gym will thrive!

At Pulse, a sense of belonging and inclusivity is promoted by the whole staff. Sure, I feel like members bond over facing challenging workouts together, but there is so much more that you can do. When someone is new, they get introduced to all the other members and become immersed. It's something our team actually trains on. We run challenges, sometimes incorporating a team element. We hold events, volleyball, flag football, sloshball, happy hour, wine night, and an annual holiday party. If you want to get your members to bond, get them drinking together. Sorry, not sorry!

I often tell new prospects that our X factor, the thing that really makes us stand out above the competition is our community. To us, everything else is just standard operating procedures. Clean facility? Check. Expert coaching? Check. Friendly professional staff? Check. Flexible schedule? Check. Follow through? Check. Holding members accountable, so they actually show up and experience how awesome we are? Check!

Your business needs to have standard operating procedures and policies in place. It needs automation. It needs systems and structure, and your team needs to be trained on all of it. Not only does it directly impact how effective your team is at handling any situation that arises, but it also empowers your team to focus on the culture of the business. When a system is created, your team will know if "A happens, I do B." "If B happens, I must do C."

Your team only has so much RAM and giving them the ability to handle any operation with autonomy through a system you implemented and trained on means their RAM is devoted towards coaching and projecting the gym's culture.

I've seen teams who are good at all the operational functions, but not good at building a strong community. I've seen teams be good at building a strong community, but not good at standard operational procedures.

Honestly, you can make a lot of mistakes and still get away with it if you have an awesome community. But, if you do everything right, that's when the gym business becomes a lot of fun! That's when you get the gym you dreamed of, and when you begin to realize that mission impossible is actually possible.

Appreciation or Depreciation

You need to understand what I'm about to say next. It doesn't matter how nice your gym is or how clean it is. It doesn't matter that you have the latest and greatest state-of-the-art equipment or the best tasting smoothies. Although all those things matter, they're not the reasons customers will continue to come to your gym.

People come to your gym because of your culture! Odds are, you aren't the only gym in town. Customers typically have numerous choices when deciding on what gym to join. You must ask yourself, "Why would they join my gym over all the others?" That's of course rhetorical; you should already know the answer. If you don't – YIKES -- figure it out! Like I said, people chose you because of your culture, but how is that culture communicated and understood by the clients? Pay attention! The only way you can communicate is through your TEAM, especially your COACHES. Your TEAM and COACHES are the business! They are your culture. If they weren't there to smile and greet members, provide a great workout session, and positively impact each person's day, you would have nothing more than an empty room full of equipment.

It's tough working in the fitness industry. Oftentimes your staff must deal with a whole bunch of "negative Nancies" that don't want to be there. Other times, it just might not be their day, but they put on a show for the members anyway. A staff that can do this needs to feel appreciated. If you have the right people in place, the best way to continue to improve and grow your business is through a deep expression of gratitude.

I cannot tell you how many times as a coach I've sat through meetings about appreciation. One of the most important elements to customer service excellence is showing appreciation. However, appreciation can't start with your staff and be directed towards your members. Appreciation needs to start at the top from the owner, and trickle down to the director and the staff, which in turn will be passed to the members.

I call this appreciation or depreciation.

As director, I cannot emphasize enough how important it is for you to say "thank you" to your staff. I try every day to tell my staff "thank you" for their hard work, for being awesome, and I always tell them how much I appreciate the job they're doing.

A team that feels appreciated will always do more than is expected of them. They'll feel like they play a critical role in the success of the business, and they'll go above and beyond to take care of the customers. The last thing I do on my way out the door is thank my front desk staff. Why? Well, not only do I genuinely appreciate the work that they do, but I also know that by thanking them, they're going to step up and take on any challenge that arises when I'm not there, and they're going to do it with a positive attitude.

If you're a gym owner or the director and you want to build a strong and LOYAL team, focus on appreciation. This means appreciation for all your staff and all the members! I often tell my clients that I love them. Is it kind of cheesy? Totally, but I do it anyway. I do love them. I do appreciate them. Their financial support is why I have a house and a car and food on the table. It's why I get to go on an occasional vacation, and why I am able to earn a living doing what I love.

You shouldn't just show gratitude towards your best or highest paying clients either. Likewise, you also shouldn't just show gratitude towards your top employee(s). What if they leave? Who will your staff and members feel loyal to if you've only expressed gratitude to one or two people? If you want them to feel loyal to you, which in turn means loyal to your business, then you need to have an outward and blatantly obvious expression of gratitude towards every player on your team. This includes all your fans -- not just the ones that have been there the longest or buy the most expensive seats.

Your staff is the business. Even an underpaid, overworked staff will continue to go above and beyond if you show them how important they are with a little effort and a ton of gratitude.

The Transition

As a gym owner, it's probably your goal to eventually be less and less involved in the day-to-day of the business, and more and more involved in overseeing from the background. While there is absolutely nothing wrong with this type of transition, it can create some definite challenges with member perception.

It's your business and if you've been involved in every aspect of it since the beginning, the members will have grown accustomed to seeing you and interacting with you on a regular basis. One of the most attractive qualities of a training studio is its small-business-feel and how accessible the owner is. As you fade into the background, members will have to adjust, and unfortunately, this type of transition can create a lot of uncertainty.

When I was promoted to Fitness Director at Pulse, Tim's other company, PROFIT, was experiencing a ton of growth. How awesome for an entrepreneur to have two flourishing businesses, right? Unfortunately, instead of just being happy for the success he was experiencing, there were a few longtime members that felt as though Tim didn't value them anymore. There was obviously nothing he did or didn't do to make them feel that way, but with the previous director leaving, me taking over, and Tim being less involved in the day to day, these members we're just trying to process all the change.

If I had known then what I know now, I easily could have squashed this and moved past it without it ever even being an issue. Unfortunately, I was new to the role and didn't recognize that these members were really just experiencing anxiety over the future of their workout sanctuary.

Gym owners may not be any less involved or invested in the business, but change; especially change that involves the owner being less present can lead to some member anxiety. Likewise, you can't tell me that some of the staff didn't feel uneasy with all the changes as well.

If you're a gym owner with the goal of transitioning away from the day to day, then understand that your members and staff may experience the same thing a select few of our members did at not fault of your own.

If you're the director, then understand that the easiest and best way to deal with this type of anxiety is through a genuine expression of appreciation. I would like to emphasize GENUINE!

Not that expressing a great deal of appreciation for your members and staff isn't always applicable, but directors need to understand how critical it is for them to be a beacon of appreciation, especially in times of change. If I had understood this as a brand new director, then I easily could have alleviated any anxiety during the transition and influenced those few members to do what they should have done in the first place; offer their support and continued loyalty.

As a director, it's critical to anticipate anxiety around any type of change or transitional period, and to be overly self-aware of how your words and actions could potentially be misinterpreted. Obviously, it can be hard to maintain that level of self-awareness when you're interacting with the same members day in and day out. The key is to proactively prevent any misinterpretation in the first place through a genuine expression of appreciation to each and every member you interact with.

Redefine and Reconnect

How can you build a community out of your trainings?

_____
_____
_____
_____
_____
_____
_____

How can you show more appreciation towards your staff and supporters?

_____
_____
_____
_____
_____
_____
_____

"To add value to others, one must first value others."

John Maxwell

Chapter 5

Retention 101

Accountability

Accountability is a big selling point, and without exception, must be built into your gym's culture.

So often in consultations, prospects tell me that they need someone to hold them accountable. When I tell them that we have a designated system within our company for that specific purpose, their eyes light up.

It's not uncommon for someone to tell me that they have a full state-of-the-art gym in their home. They always follow that statement up with, "But I never use it." My response is always the same. Without hesitation, I respond, "Pushups are free!"

It's not like I'm letting the cat out of the bag by telling you that people pay coaches to hold them accountable. If they didn't, they'd never actually do the work on their own.

Accountability is a huge issue. I would say about 80 percent of people that cancel their training memberships do so because of insufficient usage. I mean we're not some box gym taking $9.99 out of someone's bank account every month. People may not be too concerned about 10 bucks a month, but they'll pay attention to the $400 charge every month. You must be diligently monitoring gym attendance and the second a member's frequency starts to decline, you need to be on them. After all, that's what they're really paying for.

The reality is the fitness industry has been built on good intentions. There wouldn't be very many franchise gyms still in business if they only got paid per visit. Unfortunately, training gyms face a daunting challenge of not being able to skate by on good intentions. The price point is too high but having an accountability coach can help... kind of.

This is one system that has evolved over the years at Pulse. It started with one staff member being designated as the accountability coach. The job of the accountability coach was to monitor attendance and reach out to members who seemed to be falling off or not visiting as frequently as they had been previously. While the introduction of the accountability coach was a good starting place, one major flaw was that clients who didn't regularly train with the accountability coach, didn't feel accountable to them. After recognizing the system still needed improvement, I decided the accountability coach needed to be the director. After all, the director was really the initial contact for the client, and it made sense that the client would appreciate the director following through and keeping up with the member. Of course, I wasn't the director when I came up with the idea. When I took on the role of director, I quickly realized that again, members weren't super receptive to me trying to hold them accountable. There was a definite improvement, but still not the result I was looking for.

Next, I decided the solution must be for each of the coaches to act as their own accountability coach. In our team meetings, we would run a list of all the members that hadn't been in for at least a week. I then tasked the coaches with reaching out to the member based on which coach they had most often worked with. This was really the first step in the right direction, but the results still weren't where we needed them to be. In fact, every time we would reach out to a handful of members, it seemed to always result in a cancellation request.

That's the tricky thing about accountability --you want and need to hold your members accountable, but for how long? At Pulse, I noticed a trend. Certain members would fall off, then when we reached out to them, they would come back in for one or two workouts and then disappear again. Then, in an effort to do the right thing, we would reach back out to them. This cycle would occur two or three times and then the member would ask to cancel.

This is where we really started to figure out a balance between holding our members accountable, doing all we could do, and protecting the business. You see, we recognized that what we were really doing was reminding the repeat offenders that they were wasting money by not coming to the gym.

Having some real-time data and some automation definitely helped us fine tune our process. Tim and I set up accountability text and voicemail campaigns from each one of our coaches. I had each coach create three text messages and two recorded voicemails. The first message was just a standalone text that was super casual. The second was a text and a voicemail with a little more emphasis. The third was a text and a voicemail designed to come off as a 911 emergency alert.

I use Ikizmet's software because it flags members with decreased attendance. When I notice a member hasn't been in, I look to see who they last trained with and then click a button which sends out a text and/or voicemail to the client, appearing as if it was from the coach. We typically end up with a response within a few minutes.

In addition, we also recognized as a team, when we had done all we could do, but it wasn't making a bit of difference. At that point, we stopped reaching out. By not bringing it to their attention, we ended up collecting several additional months' worth of dues. While I know that sounds terrible, we are a business and running a successful business requires a lack of concern towards other people's money. More on that later though...

This latest system of accountability simplified the process, increased our ability to get ahead of the problem, and gave me more control over the whole process. Basically, it was everything we had already tried, but all combined.

With all that being said, accountability still comes down to the client/coach relationship. Sure, having a system in place, real-time data, and automation is great, but by the time you notice the warning signs, it's usually already too late. If you have a frequency problem, then you have an accountability problem; and if you have an accountability problem, then you're going to have a retention problem.

Holding members accountable should be a given, just like correcting form is a given. You wouldn't keep a coach on your team that lets members get away with poor form.

Keeping a coach on your team that doesn't hold the members accountable is just as detrimental to the business.

Like I mentioned, prospective members sit in front of me and tell me all the time that they need someone to hold them accountable. It's probably the most important value-add we have in this business. If your team accepts excuses and lets the members off the hook, then the member will quickly start to question the value of what they're paying for.

Ultimately, it doesn't matter how brilliant your programming is or how great of a gym you have, if the member isn't there to experience it, they won't see the value in it.

Frequency

Member frequency is a good indicator of the health of your business. 8x is the magic number! Statistically, members who frequent the club fewer than eight times a month are at risk of cancelling. 8x is barely twice a week, so when you think of it that way, it really makes a lot of sense that someone isn't going to get much value out of their membership if they use it less than that. Not to mention, they're also not going to see any results.

It's easy to track members who have fewer than eight visits a month with basic gym software. However, I like Ikizmet because it tracks member frequency patterns over time and then flags members when there's a drop in attendance. This system allows the user to be more proactive in identifying any type of potential issue. Eight may be the magic number, but you don't want to overlook a decline in attendance for your highest paying members that frequent the club twice as often.

I strongly believe that outside of holding members accountable, the best way to handle gym frequency is as organically as possible. That means focusing on delivering an awesome member experience, promoting a sense of community and camaraderie, having fun, and getting results. It also means positive reinforcement, which leads me to my next section.

Challenges

I really had to consider whether or not to put a section in my book about challenges. It seems like most gyms have this down. They're not hard to execute and usually the members love participating in something a little extra. However, some gyms out there are just a total mess, so I figured I'd better touch on it.

First of all, don't just come up with an idea and run with it. The worst thing you could possibly do is rollout a challenge for your members and be super unorganized. Plot and plan.

Second, come up with a challenge that supports a behavior you want your members to perform on. Reinforcing behavioral changes within a challenge is a really great way to get more buy-in from your members after the challenge ends.

For instance, if you want your members to come to the gym more, add a frequency element to the challenge. If you want members to be better about doing regular Inbody scans, include it in the challenge. If you want them to wear a heart rate monitor, include it in the challenge. Every aspect of the challenge can be a tool to reinforce the behavior you're trying to get out of your members all the time.

Third, pump it up. Start promoting at least a month ahead. Create some excitement around it and if you're charging for it, offer the members a discount for signing up early. We all know how our members love to wait until the last minute for stuff like this.

Rewards

I've spent hours just sitting in my office staring off into space. If someone were to watch me, they'd probably think I was slacking off. Really, I was racking my brain for ideas on how to get our members to do exactly what we wanted them to do. I will tell you hands down, the most effective way to get a member to do something is through a reward.

Countless meetings with the staff revolved around the questions, "How do we get our members to ____?" It seemed every single time we tried to implement something, it would start strong, pick up steam, and then die a swift death. Erin Lyons and I worked tirelessly to solve this problem and when she discovered Perkville, it was a game changer for us.

Perkville is a point rewards system that ties in with Mindbody. It rewards members automatically with points when they do whatever it is you want them to do. In other words, it allows you to determine what activities earn points and how many points each activity is worth. The points can be redeemed for whatever you decide, which honestly, our members don't care too much about. Rather, it has a pretty cool level feature where members can accumulate points to reach a new level; that next level is the real motivator. We named our levels: Bronze, Silver, Gold, Platinum, Hall of Fame, and Legend, and created a recognition board where members get their picture on the board at each level. They also get some cool branded gear each time they level up.

Outside of a Plank, I've never seen such a simple concept be so effective. Members totally obsess over getting to the next level; so much so in fact, that they were willing to pay more for stuff just because they earn extra points when they spend more.

Now there is definitely something to be said about the power of a little friendly competition, but even more to be said about rewards and recognition.

Implementing Perkville was really an eye-opener for how to manipulate our members into doing what we wanted them to. For instance:

Want members to be more proactive in scheduling classes ahead of time? Reward them with points.

Want members to check in at the front desk? Reward them with points.

Want members to come to the gym at least eight times a month? Reward them with points.

Want members to purchase a smoothie after their workout? Reward them with points.

Want members to participate in a gym challenge? Reward them with points.

Want members to pay with ACH instead of a credit card? Reward them with points.

I think you get the points, I mean point. The best part is all this happens automatically. All you have to do is set it up initially and then manage it. It's as near a complete system as possible. Sure, it's nice to offer some additional recognition and rewards every now and then to show members appreciation, but once Perkville is up and running, it's pretty hands-off from a tracking perspective. Though, I do recommend putting a front desk staff person or coach in charge of managing it, especially if you have a levels board.

Content Kings

This is what I call accessibility and it's often a missing piece of the member experience. Accessibility is basically how convenient it is for the member to approach any of the team and the comfort of doing so. It's a perception or expression to the members that we're here for them and they can ask us anything. That's not all, though. Accessibility has a subliminal message; a message of status or inclusivity and perk that only members of our elite club have access to.

Building accessibility into your member experience requires internal and external elements. The internal is easy. It's a personal touch and communication. Your team can perform on it by simply walking up to the member and letting them know that it's okay for them to reach out anytime they need anything. It's, "Here's my number, call or text anytime you have questions." Some members will act on it and some won't, but that's why the next step is a personal phone call or text to the member, to follow up. It's a simple text that says, "Hey, just wanted to follow up from our conversation earlier. Text me if you need anything. Great chatting with you!"

That's really it. If every member of your team does that, you'll be able to address any concern before it becomes an issue, because they'll feel comfortable enough to bring it up.

External accessibility requires way more work, but it's a necessary evil. There are 168 hours in a week. Out of those, how many does the typical member spend in the gym? Four, five, or six at most. It's guaranteed that the member has a lot going on those other 162 hours, and if you don't stay in front of them when they're outside the gym, they'll lose focus, and you'll lose them. As if it's not already challenging enough to deliver a great experience to the same people every single day in person, the experience must continue once they leave.

It's one thing to use content for marketing, it's another to use it for engagement, community, culture, and retention. One of the mistakes I made was not prioritizing this earlier on. When you're putting out great content to attract clients, but not overwhelming your existing clients with fresh, exciting content, you're doing it wrong.

How often have you met and signed up a brand-new client who seems pumped to get going? Then, a couple weeks or months later, they stop showing up, they won't return your calls or texts, and then they send you a cancelation request? This is quite common in the industry, especially at the start of a new year. It's partly a mindset issue, but it's also a content issue.

Notice, I said not prioritizing earlier on? As a new director, it didn't take long for me to recognize the importance of putting out mass amounts of content for the members. The idea had existed long before I even started working at Pulse. The problem was my team had a bad attitude about it. They were training and taking care of the members in front of them, and they thought that was enough. Anything else and I was just giving them extra work to do; extra work they didn't think they were getting paid for.

I challenge you to get on Instagram and start scrolling... It won't take you very long to come across a billion trainer/fitness models putting out content. Your clients are going to be looking at and influenced by someone else's content. If your coaching staff were independent, they would be doing the same thing for themselves. A negative attitude towards doing it for your gym is not an attitude you need or want on your team.

DIRECTING FITNESS

The only way you can compete in today's overabundance of content is by putting out your own great content and overwhelming your clients with it. As Fitness Director, I focus more on the content going out to our members and Tim focuses on the content going out to attract new members because that's what he's an expert at and helps other gym owners with on an international level. This Director/Owner relationship works exceptionally well at Pulse and as a director, I highly suggest you prioritize putting out content for your existing members.

Why do you think Coca-Cola and Pepsi still have commercials? Why do they buy up billboard space? Why do they run advertisements and sponsor celebrities and sporting events? Doesn't everyone already know about their brands? Does anyone even pay attention to their ads? Since millions of people already buy their products every single day, what positive financial impact do their ads even have?

Retention and relevance are a closely knit team. Your retention will improve organically by putting out more genuine, relevant content from the team that is specifically directed towards your existing clients. Sure, you still need content directed toward attracting new members, but don't neglect your existing members. Pulse has a Facebook page that is public and a Facebook group that is private, exclusively for members. Both have different posting strategies. Obviously, the public page is more focused on attraction. The private page is focused on -- you guessed it -- culture, community, and appreciation.

Avoid using your community page as just an announcement board or a place to pitch members. For instance, if all you do is make posts about discounted supplements and classes being cancelled, you won't get a lot of engagement. I'm not saying you can't use it for that, but if that's all you use it for, you'll create a negative member perception.

Content must be built into your internal culture; and although your team must understand and participate in putting out genuine content, it still needs a strategy. Don't just go about it haphazardly, because then, you definitely won't get the buy-in you're looking for from the team. Design a structure and systematic approach to it. Have coaches alternate writing blogs and schedule weekly posting responsibilities for each team member. I like one scheduled post and one random post.

Thanks to Tim building a podcast studio and starting the "Built To Grow Podcast," my team ended up with a unique opportunity to start our own podcast, "Healthy Living Scottsdale." In my experience, the podcast is one of the best content strategies you can utilize, because it acts as a hybrid. Not only is it a great content for the members, it also gives prospects an insider sneak peak of how we operate. More importantly, it gave my team a better understanding of the importance and necessity of putting out great content. The podcast didn't just come by itself either; with it, we started a podcast Instagram page and Facebook page.

I mentioned overwhelming your members with content. Yes, overwhelm them! Give them too much to process. Send the experience home with them. Deliver your culture, sense of community, and elite status to them through their phones. Maybe they'll look at every tenth post and that's totally fine. No matter what, you just have to stay in front of them, appeal to them, stay relevant, and stay genuine. Coca-Cola and Pepsi don't need to advertise to get new customers. They advertise to stay in the forefront of people's minds and create loyalty.

Overwhelm your audience with content, don't overwhelm your team. After what I just described, that might seem impossible, but it's not. There can be a lot of overlap with content.

I like a general macro theme with micro themes. For instance, decide for the next month that all your content on every page is going to be about nutrition. Nutrition is your macro theme; it's big and broad. Then divide up your content with smaller more detailed information about nutrition. One week your content can be about meal prep. The next week can be about eating for your body type. The following week, it could be about tracking macros. These are all micro themes under your macro theme of nutrition. It's an easy strategy that your team can keep track of, and you can use all the same information with slight differences to engage your members or attract prospects. In other words, systemize your content strategy.

DIRECTING FITNESS

Redefine and Reconnect

Design a strategy for turning your training into a community:

ZACHARY J. COLUMBIA

"When people talk, listen completely."

Ernest Hemingway

Chapter 6

If You Build It, They Will Stay

Staffing

Determining your staffing needs and positions is one of the most critical elements to having a highly functioning business. The unfortunate reality is, most gym owners hire because they need help, not because they've created a new position -- and there is a definitive difference.

It's a big mistake to hire reactively just because there isn't enough manpower to get everything done. Be proactive in setting up the systems that the business runs on and create positions around operating those systems. Sure, it's important to identify job duties that need to get done, but creating a specific role around each one of the systems that runs the business is really the first step in building a strong team.

How are you going to advertise, interview, qualify, hire, and train someone if you aren't even sure what you need them for? Many gym owners and directors do this, and then end up frustrated when they aren't getting what they need out of their new hire. Start with the system and then hire into that system. Be proactive, not reactive!

It's definitely an important responsibility of the director to identify potential staffing needs. Data and intuition can be used to determine when a new position needs to be created. It's called business acumen and the deciding factor is, how will a new position create more revenue?

It's not just new positions that we need to pay attention to however, but also to replacements. Turnover in the fitness industry is extreme to say the least, and the director should never be blindsided by a team member deciding to leave. Openness and communication are incredibly important in the director role and being in tune with what's happening with each team member is necessary.

I've seen a lot of shooting stars in my time as a director. A shooting star burns high and bright and then OUT! I've interviewed, hired, and trained both coaches and support staff that I thought were amazing. They put on a great show for several months, or maybe even a year. They were the brightest stars in the room, until they weren't!

No matter how great you think an employee is, you can never -- I repeat, YOU CAN NEVER -- get too comfortable. Always stay one step ahead. Always have a contingency plan for not if, but for when they burn out. Be aware, because the second you start having issues with your all-star that never gave you any trouble before, that is when they are headed out the door.

Yes, be proactive when it comes to staffing, but also be proactive in protecting and safeguarding the clients and the business. That way when they leave or you must ask them to leave, it has a minimal impact on the members.

I wish that was all there was to say regarding staffing, but we didn't cover the best part yet. By best, I mean the absolute worst ever.

If you could clone yourself and have a team of "you" filling every role and managing every aspect of the business, not only would you have no problems ever, but you'd also have the Microsoft, Google, or Apple of gyms. You'd have so many members and so much money, you'd be turning business away. No, I'm not talking about your abilities or knowledge. We all know that having a diverse team with different perspectives and expertise ultimately makes the team better. What I mean is one simple, realistic, yet hard-to-grasp fact for gym owners -- no one will work as hard for someone as they'll work for themselves!

There are few things more important for a business owner than who they trust their business with, and this is exactly why. No matter the integrity or work ethic of the individual, they simply don't have the investment in the business that the owner has. If every single member of the team was as bought-in and vested in the business as the owner, the business would have no choice other than to flourish. That simply isn't the reality and it never will be. Understand, the lower an employee on the totem pole, the less vested in the business. As an owner or director, staying an hour late may not be any big deal, but to a coach, it's a big deal. They may do it, but they'll also probably complain about it and expect additional compensation.

If a team member goes above and beyond on their own, never miss the opportunity to recognize and reward them. Afterall, they're doing something not required of them and showing that they're invested in the success of the business. Reinforce that behavior (more on that in a bit).

It's important to note, the director should really just be an extension or as near a clone as possible of the owner. They should always treat the business as their own. If you're a director, you need this mindset in order to be successful. If you're a gym owner, you should always seek out the individual with the character necessary to take care of your business. Even if that means investing the time and energy to train and polish someone who lacks the know-how but has the right attitude and work ethic.

      The director needs to share this understanding when it comes to determining staffing needs, interviewing, onboarding, training, and developing their team. There are few things as rewarding as receiving positive feedback from clients about team performance. On the contrary, there are few things that can make life as miserable for the director as when you have a poor performing team or a team that doesn't seem invested in the success of the business. It's really difficult to know how someone is going to turn out just from the interview process. For example, no one ever comes out and openly admit they only want a short-term job to pay the bills on their way to something better. However, statistics show that's the norm in the industry and it's pretty evident if you pay attention. Coaches are a dime a dozen. If you don't feel like a coach is cutting it or has a bad attitude, just replace them. It's your job as the director to protect the business, and if you let a bad coach linger, the clients will end up leaving. If you get rid of a bad coach, they may take a few clients with them, but most will appreciate the fact that you had their best interest in mind.

The next section is about the team perspective and how to keep your team focused and motivated, but before we get into that, we need to talk about a unique challenge we face today, Millennials.

Millennial Matters

There's quite a bit of information out there on how to effectively manage Millennials, which is helpful because the fitness industry has been flooded with a millennial workforce. I want to share my wisdom and experience in how to manage them, specifically in the industry. Prepare for my rant... I mean perspective.

First off, I'm a millennial and I have to tell you, my generation's way of thinking is messed up. You hear a lot about the sense of entitlement. Does it exist? Yes, but it's not the foundational issue. Our parents and grandparents did not share their struggles with us. We saw all the good things, the wealth, the success, the material things. No one told us there was a time when our grandparents worked 60 hours a week and took home $75. We didn't see it, and no one wanted to tell us about it.

"How much does dad make?" "$100k a year." "If you go to college, get a good education and work hard, you'll get there too."

DIRECTING FITNESS

We took that as, when we graduated and got a job, we'd start out making $75k, $80k a year. We didn't realize we would be making $30k and working really hard for the next 20 years to get there. Our parents didn't tell us that and we only saw the success. That's problem number one.

Problem number two is the internet. Millennials are the first generation to grow up with access to everything. What did we see? People getting unbelievably rich on the internet. Now, we have an up and coming generation that thinks they're all going to be self-made millionaires because they have Instagram. This is especially true in our industry. It's where we get the independent trainer mindset and it's the absolute worst thing you can have in your gym.

As a director, you will never be able to lead the business to the next level if you have employees that function independently or are trying to build a brand for themselves outside of your gym. Most coaches don't realize how difficult it actually is to run a successful training business. They see fame and fortune falsely sold on social media by online coaches and think they can do it all by themselves. Since they don't recognize the work the owner has or is putting in, they don't value the fact that the facility is being financed, licensing fees and taxes are being paid, and thousands are being spent on marketing and software infrastructure. They don't value the fact that someone is doing the sales, someone is managing, someone is cleaning, someone is answering the phone. They don't value the fact that the gym owner risked it all to start their business in the first place and they definitely won't value the director working hard to bring it all together and function seamlessly. They simply don't get it!

I went to a great deal of effort in earlier chapters to explain the complexities and challenges of being a coach. Almost every gym owner and director out there has been a coach. They have the luxury of understanding the position firsthand, but how many coaches have been a director or gym owner? Just like with the example of our parents and grandparents, coaches don't see the struggle, the risk, and the sweat equity that it took and takes to run a profitable gym.

I believe the key to managing Millennials is this, "If you tell them, they'll forget. If you show them, they'll know. If you involve them, they'll understand."

Recognize that Millennials want to be involved, but most won't take initiative on their own to get involved. As director, it can be really challenging to devote time out of your busy schedule to involve and include the coaches in aspects of the business that extend beyond their normal responsibilities. However, it's incredibly important in having a cohesive, dedicated team. Appreciation or depreciation is a two-way street and the best way to get the team to appreciate the hard work and sacrifice that goes into running the company that pays their salary, is by involving them so they understand.

Team Perspective

Pulse is a studio with a semi-private training model. All the coaches are salaried employees, and from my point of view, the coaches have it pretty great. They don't have to go out and get clients, all they have to do is show up to work, smile, and provide a great workout and member experience. They have a set schedule and members book themselves in on an app. I even design the programming for them. It's exactly what 99.999% of coaches thought being a personal trainer was all about before realizing it's more of a sales job.

Regardless, over the years I've experienced plenty of complaining about the team not making enough money or being asked to do too much. One of the main complaints was that whether they trained one person an hour or six people, they got paid the same. Again, the coaches were living life in 50-minute increments. Their perspective was totally different.

If you're a gym owner or fitness director and you're reading this, a semi-private model with salaried coaches totally makes sense to you. That's because it's absolutely the best model in the industry! It's the most affordable for the client and the most profitable and sustainable for the gym owner. However, if you're an independent trainer, it probably is not! There's a disconnect. If a coach gets paid whether they are training one client, six clients, or zero clients, there isn't much incentive for them to work harder. Plus, we know that not all clients are created equal. Some are totally awesome to work with and some are a nightmare.

When I first joined Pulse Fitness, I would see clients schedule with a certain coach. Then, the coach would move that client off their schedule and onto my schedule. It wasn't long before I realized that the fun clients were getting pulled off of my schedule and replaced with the not-so-fun ones by my coworkers. It would have been easy to change the settings in our software to prevent coaches from moving clients around, but that wouldn't address the underlying issue.

Do yourself a favor; make a list with your best clients on one side and you're most challenging on the other side. Track how long they last. I can tell you what you'll find -- the clients that aren't much fun to train won't last anywhere near as long as the fun ones. Why? From your coach's perspective, there is nothing in it for them to deliver the same experience as the fun clients get. REALIZE THAT I said, "From the coach's perspective." You're the business owner or director. You see green. Not to make you sound greedy, but your perspective is different. You're paying the coach a salary to perform on certain responsibilities. Your expectation is set, but I'm telling you on behalf of your coaches, because I saw it when I was a coach, there's a disconnect. Remember, we just laid out what a coach's day and each 50-minute segment looks like. Your coaches are going to get tired and they're going to naturally gravitate towards the easier, more enjoyable clients.

This story will probably sound familiar to you: When I took over as fitness director and became the person signing up each member, retention became a top priority of mine. Selling has never come natural to me and each member I signed up was a big deal. The ones I signed up at the end of a twelve-hour day were an even bigger deal. A lot of effort went into getting them to join and I expected a lot of effort to go into keeping them. I realized that without an incentive to go above and beyond for each and every member, coaches would continue to deliver a different level of service to different members. As a coach, it was challenging for me to just be salaried. I wanted more opportunities. I knew I was doing a great job and working hard to provide a superior level of service. I wanted to do more and be rewarded for it and assumed my peers wanted the same.

A huge dilemma with our model and a salaried coaching staff was figuring out how to create buy-in and incentives without encouraging the independent trainer mindset. After all, our model relied on members being able to work with any coach and receive the same consistent experience, regardless of who was training them.

To combat this, when I became the director, I set up a quarterly capacity bonus for coaches. Our semi-private model allowed coaches to train five clients per session. If a coach trained at 60% capacity, they received 50 cents per client they had trained throughout the quarter, 70% capacity and they received 60 cents, 80% and they got 70 cents, and 90%... well no one ever hit 90%.

I thought this system was brilliant because as I mentioned, I was motivated, worked hard, and would have loved to be incentivized. Two years after implementing this bonus structure, we only had one coach that would regularly bonus, and retention hadn't really improved all that much.

You must understand, not everyone functions the same. The coach that consistently bonused, was more like you and me. They had an entrepreneurial mindset and it motivated them. However, as director, it wasn't enough for me to just say, "Here you go team, I created this bonus structure for you, now go perform." I think it's safe to say that everyone wants to be rewarded financially, but not everyone understands how to get there and not everyone is motivated to put in the extra work to get there.

I've heard it said of the industry, that if you ask a trainer to do too much, you'll be disappointed. Well, I don't think that's really true. In reality, they already do a lot, even if all they have to do is provide a great workout for the members. The problem is most trainers are stuck in the box and can't get far enough outside to see the big picture. Their world is training and that's what they know. Keeping that in mind, the only realistic approach is creating a TEAM focused mindset.

We all refer to our staff as a team, but are they really? Teams share a common goal. What common goal does your team share? If I asked you that question, would you give me the, "I want to lose weight and tone up" answer that we so often hear in consultations? That's not a goal! You wouldn't accept that answer from a client, so don't give it to your team!

Everyone in this industry knows the S.M.A.R.T. goal model: Specific, Measurable, Attainable, Relevant, and Time-based. Why is it the go-to for our clients when we want them to accomplish something, but not our own team? If you want to bridge the gap between gym owner/director and staff, you need SMART goals!

Now back to TEAM! In team sports, individual performance directly correlates to overall team performance. There is no disconnect. Everyone understands it, clear and simple. Therefore, it really shouldn't be rocket science to understand that you need to reward the INDIVIDUAL and the TEAM.

The capacity bonus rewarded the individual, but it didn't reward the team, nor did it establish a common goal. Once I realized why the gap hadn't been filled, the problem was easily solved in 3 simple steps.

Create a SMART team goal that makes sense for your gym and incentivize.

I like the idea of setting a goal each month for total monthly sales revenue. It impacts the team as a whole. From membership sales to retention, to smoothies and supplement sales, to challenges. Everyone's performance has a direct impact on the number. It's monthly, which is a short enough timeframe for the team to stay focused and it obviously aligns with the goals of the business.

Create individual goals that support your team goal and incentivize.

In our case, this was the capacity bonus. Honestly, it solved a lot of issues for us. Coaches were incentivized to fill up their schedules. It encouraged delivering a great experience so people would come back. Its increased accountability to make sure clients scheduled (and showed up) for their next workout. And since we had the individual goal and the team goal, if a client needed to come in at a different time and train with a different coach, it was encouraged because they were still going to be incentivized for accomplishing the TEAM Goal!

Take your team by the hand and show them step-by-step how to accomplish both goals.

This one is definitely the most difficult to accomplish. Why? If your team was capable of going out and accomplishing these goals on their own, they would be running their own gym. Even if you create a SMART goal and a supporting individual goal with incentives, your team probably won't know how to get there on their own. Make these criteria for hiring staff? Smart thinking, but the concern here is that person will leave and take your clients with them. You'll just be a launching pad for that individual. It's better to hire a loyal coach with potential, who can be taught and mentored, no matter how time-consuming on your part.

Obviously, holding your team's hand and teaching them how to perform to accomplish both goals requires a certain expertise that you might not have. Not to worry, this book is called Directing Fitness after all.

Staff Training & Development

I've always tried to avoid the corporate feel. Like everyone else, I hate cheesy training that feels robotic and that employees dread. It's noticeably brutal, especially when you have a small staff with 5-10 employees. When I started out as director, I thought the secret was to simply hire the right person with the right characteristics and everything would run smoothly. While that's partially true, we in the fitness industry, don't have the luxury of relying on one or two individual performers. As I already mentioned, the nature of the fitness beast requires an impossible level of consistency and perfection. This is especially true in a semi-private training environment where members interact with different coaches. Your team might be made up of awesome players, but if each of them is running a different play, you'll never score a touchdown. Your team needs to be on the same page of the playbook, and they need to practice running the plays until they can get it right every time.

Individuality is great and having different personalities broadens your appeal. However, member experience excellence requires consistency and standardization. That's the uniqueness and challenge of bringing together any group of individuals to accomplish a common goal. Don't fool yourself into thinking that just because you hire great candidates, they'll all be able to unify and function.

I've also learned that rousing speeches and talking points aren't enough. No matter your delivery, the message isn't enough to create change, buy in, or improved performance. Frankly, you just can't bring it all together without training and development.

The best way I can describe this to anyone who is like me and hates the idea of corporate training, is through sports. Athletes don't just walk out on the field and perform; they practice, they learn, they develop. Teams don't just win championships; they practice, they bond, they overcome together. Athletes don't stop practicing once they've made the team. Instead, they practice and train together to make the team stronger. As cheesy as it may seem to role play or practice with your team, it's no different than with sports. Sure, the game's a little bit different, but winning is still the goal.

Practice answering the phone. Practice giving tours. Practice greetings and smiling. Practice answering questions and addressing customer complaints. Practice starting and ending on time. Practice, practice, practice.

At Pulse, we have our core values and what we refer to as "The Standard." Our standard is a list of 10 checkpoints that make up our member experience. It's what every visit to Pulse should include. We also have a standard for our workouts, which breaks down five check items that every workout should entail. For your team, you must look at it as a sport – explain and present it that way. Keep in mind that there is nothing worse for a team than a prima donna that thinks they're too good to practice. You don't want to root for those athletes on TV, and you certainly don't want them on your team. No one is above practice, no matter how good they are.

    Determine what your core values are and what your standard is. Relate them back to the impact on member experience. Make performing on them your team's number one responsibility and manage off them. Don't worry about retention, don't worry about sales revenue. Instead, focus on your standard. Train on it. Practice it! If you know for a fact that your standard and core values are on point, then the only thing your team needs to worry about is execution. It's easy for them and it's easy to manage. If a checkpoint gets missed, the director or owner can jump in, point it out, and correct it. It's not personal, it's just the performance expectation. It's literally THE STANDARD!

    Finally, systemization and automation are important, as they help prevent human error. Incorporate these into your training. Automate what you can and systemize the rest for your team. Make checklists and train your staff to check the boxes. Nothing needs to be harder than it should be, so keep it simple.

Onboarding & Setting Expectations

Onboarding new hires is one of the most difficult challenges you'll face as director. In and of itself, introducing and training a new member of the team isn't that bad. On the other hand, onboarding a new hire while trying to keep up with 500 million other responsibilities is! If you've ever done this, then you know the struggle. Almost everything else has to stop for a week, so that you can be 100% devoted to onboarding. Then, you must set aside numerous hours over the next several weeks to continue training and development. I wish that I had some special wisdom to impart on you that would allow you to keep up with all your daily responsibilities and effectively train a new team member, but it's really just about sweat equity.

The worst mistake you can make is not investing enough time and effort into a new member of your team. I completely and utterly understand the challenge, but it's worth the investment in the long run. Thankfully, I've learned that having a new hire shadow the director as they go about their daily responsibilities is just as important as having them shadow the coaches and support staff. It lays the foundation for the effort and attention to detail that your business requires, while also building respect for the position.

Remember, having the staff understand the director's role creates both respect and appreciation. I use any pressing issue that needs to be addressed as a teaching opportunity. Doing so allows me to keep up with the absolute necessities while all my time and effort is being devoted to onboarding. It's a good plan in theory, but in reality, you'll also have to put in extra hours after a new hire leaves for the day to get everything else done.

On day one, I show a new hire the ropes. Where everything is and what they have access to use. We fill out paperwork, set up software and email accounts, go through our employee handbook word for word, and review core values and our member experience standard. Everything I go over with them is tied back to our member experience, community, and culture. It's serious business, but I do my best to make it fun, joke around, and laugh. Then, we'll get them out on the floor to shadow a training session or two, meet a few members, and start understanding how our workouts are structured and programmed before wrapping up for the day. This is done regardless of whether they're a coach or in a different position. No matter what, it's important to have your team understand every role in the company and shadow all of the positions. I even suggest having them hang with the owner for a day if you can make it happen logistically.

Day two starts with a review of what we covered on day one, and dives deeper into our standard and core values. We train a little more on how to use our software and systems, but really focus in on our business structure and how we function. It's about understanding the importance of the TEAM and how everyone plays a critical role in the success of the business.

Then, if they're a coach, we get them out on the floor to shadow again. If they're front desk or support staff, they shadow at the front desk. If I have consultations scheduled, I always have the new team member sit in with me. That way, they learn what's involved in getting a new member, and what expectations I set that our team must perform on.

Day three is a reinforcement of days one and two, especially when it comes to the member experience. The new hire will spend several hours shadowing at the front desk, regardless of their position. The front desk is a great place to interact with and get to know the members. It's also important for a coach to understand the whole experience flow, from greeting, to working out, to walking out the front door. As a team, we control and lead the client through their whole visit. It's also important in a small business for everyone to be able to step in and cover where there is a need. Cross-training does this and that is exactly what we're trying to accomplish.

Day four and day five, the focus becomes shadowing with increasing responsibility and reinforcement, with follow up and continuing explanation. It's several hours of shadowing me and the other team members. We end the day with a Q & A. I ask questions, they answer, and they ask questions and I answer.

The next week is what we at Pulse refer to as reverse shadowing. The new hire puts into practice what they've learned, and the rest of the staff takes turns shadowing them. We guide them through and give them instruction and pointers along the way. Once we decide they've got it down and they're performing at the same level as the rest of the team, (there is no set time to how long that will be; it's usually about a week though), we'll turn them loose… sort of.

Once we feel confident that they have it, I observe from a distance. At our gym we have a two-way mirror, which allows me to sit in the office and watch training sessions without it feeling like I'm hovering. I can see the front desk from my office, so those team members know I'm always watching. My system at this point becomes self-evaluation vs. my evaluation. The team member is given a checklist of "Our Standard," which outlines the main areas they are expected to perform on. They evaluate their own performance with me, as I evaluate their performance. Any discrepancy or area of performance that wasn't up to par gets discussed and further trained on.

If you're already regularly holding practices with your staff, then all of your training materials should be in place for onboarding new team members. It's important that you have this, because inconsistencies in training mean inconsistencies in staff performance and the member experience moving forward. Your new hire should undergo the same training your existing team already experienced. You shouldn't have the attitude of "this time you're going to get it right." If your existing team doesn't already have it right, your new hire will quickly forget everything you taught them in the onboarding process and perform at the same level as your existing team.

There is nothing easier than having a checklist of expectations, communicating how performing on them impacts the business, and training on them -- REPEATEDLY! It makes onboarding simple, effective, and the best part is, it's straightforward to manage day in and day out.

Just a side note: don't micromanage your team. Make sure they got it. Make sure they're performing each and every day. Revisit and reinforce occasionally, but if they're doing a good job, let them be. There is nothing worse for a go-getter or a high performing team member who is consistently going above and beyond, than being micromanaged. Teach. Train. Trust!

Commission-Based Services

One message that I've always tried to express to the team is that the sky's the limit when it comes to what you can do with your career at Pulse. The key phrase here, is at Pulse.

As I discussed in the Millennial Matters section, staff members can struggle to recognize the opportunities that come from being a part of a team. They think all that's required to build an empire is access to social media, so they consider going at it alone. Any gym owner or director understands this is far from reality. However, if you can create an environment that gives your coaches the opportunity to progress in a way that benefits the business and themselves, you can avoid conflicts of interest.

The entrepreneurial mindset is a tremendous plus to have on your team and giving your staff the opportunity to own a service within the business can be mutually beneficial. Whether it be nutrition coaching, behavioral change and development, or massage therapy, giving your coaches an additional revenue stream allows the coach to further develop their careers and provides the members with an added service. It can mean more revenue for the business and the coach already has a captive audience to market to. It's a total win/win as long as the services align with the business and core values.

Having an additional revenue stream for the team is a great way to attract talented coaches. It's something I always highlight as a perk during the interview process. I actually do this at Pulse myself. I have specialized training in Neuromuscular Soft Tissue Release and started providing this service to our members before being promoted to director. I still do a few treatments each week and enjoy the isolated interaction with the members.

As director, I'm always happy to offer my support to anyone that's looking to learn more, do more, and get paid more. However, I'm just there for guidance, not to do the work or convince the owner to provide any sort of financial backing. If the coach wants to build something, then they need to prove it with their own financial support and sweat equity.

We've had several different models over the years at Pulse, but since coaches are building off of an already existing business and audience, I suggest a 50/50 commission split that's independent and performed on outside regular paid hours. In my experience, this is the cleanest and easiest model to track.

Team Rewards

When it comes to rewards, there is no difference between your members and your team! If you want your team to perform at the level you expect, reinforce those performance areas with incentives and rewards. Just like offering rewards to steer your members in the right direction, you can create buy-in from your team through incentives. It's important to understand that it doesn't always need to be a financial reward either.

There is a difference in perspective from a business owner or high-level manager to a grunt-level employee. Oftentimes, some brilliant new idea isn't looked at as being such; especially if it's going to create more work for your staff. Buy-in may not end up being what you want it to be. Incentives can certainly help, but you also must remember that the workforce mindset is different now than it used to be.

Millennials have a totally different perspective than generations past. The "if I work harder, I'll earn more," mindset isn't prevalent with the current generation. The reward is practically expected before earned. It's the, "everyone gets a trophy" attitude. It's not necessarily a bad thing, it's just different, which means you have to reward differently.

Having rewards and incentives being inherent within your company's culture is great. Depending on the size of your team, you could have an employee of the month that wins a prize or a paid day off. (Millennials love days off). You could do a monthly raffle for your team where they receive an entry every time they perform on a specific criterion and at the end, whoever's name is drawn gets a prize. You could also establish a monthly revenue goal and give bonuses or gift cards to your whole team if they hit that goal. Rewards and incentives like these require a little creativity and their success really depends on your team dynamic.

Rewarding and incentivizing your team is a way to increase performance and create loyalty from within. Ask yourself, what perks does an employee receive outside of a paycheck. If you have poor performing employees, you won't really feel like rewarding them and giving them extra perks. However, having these things in place is a great way to attract and keep the best talent.

Building Your Dream Team

Ultimately, what you are really trying to accomplish by building a highly functioning, highly motivated team, is business growth and sustainability. This business requires too much for one man or one woman. The one-man show doesn't work for a training studio. (That's why independent trainers pay rent instead of owning their own facility.) The thought process around creating positions, hiring, onboarding, training, and rewarding the team must revolve around the end user and finally the success of the business. If you build it, not only will the members come -- they'll stay.

DIRECTING FITNESS

Redefine and Reconnect

How are you going to build your dream team?

"The function of leadership is to produce more leaders, not more followers."

Ralph Nader

Chapter 7

Systemization & Optimization

Systematic Approach

One of the primary reasons for the downfall of many training gyms is that they're not organized. I don't mean organized in the sense that they stack papers or don't have consistent schedules. I mean that they don't approach day-to-day operations systematically, which inevitably leads to inconsistencies in management of both clients and staff members. Our industry requires too much of a human element not to work off systems and standard operating procedures.

However, establishing these for the personal trainer who's become a director or gym owner can be quite challenging.

If you're a gym owner, think about how amazing it would be to walk through the front door of your gym at 9am and instantly fill the energy. You get pumped to be there and you serve up a high-five to your front desk staff. The music is bumping, the place smells great, looks clean, and you hear your coaches bring the fire. As you stroll into your office, members stop and wave at you, feeling grateful for giving them a place of belonging. Then you fire up your MacBook, hop on Facebook and make an inspirational post for all your members. Next, you briefly glance at your finances, but everything looks strong and there's plenty of money in the bank, so you strategize on where to take your business next.

Sounds like a great morning at "You Fitness," right? That dream is possible to achieve with the right systems in place and the right director to oversee it all.

I'm so grateful to have stepped into a director role under a business owner who actually specializes in building systems for gyms. There was so much already established to function off of and build upon. That's what a great director does -- they manage the systems, the staff who use the systems, and they continue to improve and build upon the systems.

Simply put, taking a systematic approach is the most efficient, the most consistent, and the most effective way of running a business. You can train your team to execute seamlessly while easily managing and tracking them. It's impossible for anyone to do everything themselves and it's definitely the wrong approach to expect your team to do things the right way without having a designated plan in place. If everyone is left up to their own discretion, the business will suffer.

If I called your gym at 8am to ask a question and then called back at 8pm to ask the same question, would I get two different answers? If I spoke to two different people, would they answer the phone differently? Does the member experience change depending on what staff members you have working? If I came into the gym and got a tour from two different staff members would they follow the same format and provide the same information?

If you're not entirely confident in the answers to these questions as they pertain to your gym, then there's room for improvement.

A systematic approach allows your staff to follow the same rules and respond the same exact way for every possible scenario universally. It simplifies the business. It prevents human error and it allows you to manage the people who run the systems by simply looking to see what was done.

Transparent systems are the best. As director, I don't like to waste time. I like for everyone to know what's going on, whose responsibility it is, and who did what. If a step was missed, then you know it. You know who missed it, and you can correct it. This is how gym owners hold their director accountable without being involved in every insignificant detail and it's how directors can effectively manage without micromanaging. Side note: your team can feel empowered by making improvements to the systems. Reward that!

Since I think you get the point, I want to illustrate a few of the systems I use on a regular basis and explain why they're necessary. Before we do that though, it's important to understand how to assess the effectiveness of your standard operating procedures and systems, while identifying where improvements can be made.

Data Driven

As you already saw from my diagram, I like to use data to better understand what areas need improving. Many gym owners out there don't recognize how important data really is for steering their business in the right direction. If the gym owner isn't focused on the numbers, how can they expect their director to be? "It's just a gym," is not the right perspective to have when it comes to analysis and the financial success of the business. You need to dive deeply into the data to understand your flaws and come up with profitable solutions.

For example:

You could easily let someone out of an annual contract and not put up much of a fight because you're afraid of a negative review. I completely understand your point of view. However, early on in my role as director, I pulled up a report that showed me how much money we didn't collect on terminated annual contracts over a 5-year period, and it was over $80k. $80k! What could your business do with an extra $80k!?

How about membership freezes? Because Scottsdale is so seasonal, we allowed members to freeze their memberships whenever they wanted. For us, the question of being able to freeze a membership during the summer was a much bigger issue during the sales consultation, than an annual contract ever was. However, because we were so flexible with our freeze policy, members would go on freeze for three or four months and then contact us asking to cancel a week before their membership was set to begin billing again. How do you enforce a 30-day cancellation policy or an annual contract with someone that hasn't set foot in your business in several months? The answer is: you don't. At least not without it being settled in the court of public opinion on Yelp or Google Reviews. We found that nearly 40% of our members that went on freeze, never came back.

Another major problem that our business faced due to the seasonal nature of Scottsdale, was a drastic drop in recurring revenue during the summer months. Think about this: as a business, you want to charge as much as the customer is willing to pay. In Scottsdale, the customer that leaves for four, five, or six months out of the year can afford to pay the most. Raise your prices and you alienate the hard-working full-time resident who can't afford a second home. Lower your prices, and you don't collect what you could have collected from the higher paying members.

If you have a business that is influenced by the seasons, then you're definitely going to have different staffing demands at different points throughout the year. For us, the questions are always: How many coaches do we need? How many training hours are necessary? Should we shrink our schedule or cut our hours?

Without data, you can't make these decisions confidently with an understanding that you're doing what's right for the business. Actually, you probably wouldn't even be able to identify that there was a problem in the first place. My recommendation is to track everything. When in doubt, make an Excel worksheet for everything.

Leads to members, worksheet. Memberships by types, worksheet. Training hours available vs. filled, worksheet. Expenses, worksheet. Smoothies sold vs. member visits, worksheet.

You get the point. Input data and pay attention to trends. Trust me, you'll identify many areas needing improvement that you thought were doing perfectly fine. Data is king. If you don't know the solution to a problem, always ask, "What do the numbers say?"

Microeconomics of The Gym

Microeconomics are the key to maximizing profit, and the concept is super easy to understand. Here's how you leverage it in the training business.

First, collect some data. How many members are you training at 5am? How much does it cost you to staff at 5am? If you make more training during that hour than it costs you to be open, obviously you would want to stay open. If it costs you more, then you may want to eliminate that hour of service. Obviously, there are some other factors that come into play, such as your ability to grow, but ultimately, it's all just math.

How much do you make on a one-on-one training hour vs. a semi-private training hour vs. a class? I can tell you right now, the semi-private is going to be the most profitable, but could you attract more members for a class during a slow training hour, or should you scrap a class to add availability for a more profitable semi-training?

For gym owners, do you know what the right amount of square footage is for your business to maximize profit? What is your cost per square foot? How many members can you fit into the space vs. how many members you're realistically going to have?

There's a sweet spot that will maximize profit. I understand that most directors aren't working on a new buildout, but you should still figure out a way to make the most profit out of the square footage you have. Sometimes that may be a sublease to someone that can act as a referral partner or something like Tim did at Pulse with building a podcast studio.

These are the types of things that directors should be analyzing. Without data, without crunching the numbers, you're missing out on profit. Compile the data and analyze it, while considering both the impact on the members and the bottom line. The status quo isn't good enough. If you go back to the decision wheel, then you understand that the data and impact on both the members and staff should be taken into consideration in the decision-making process.

As director, if I'm not making a major change, I just make the call and roll with it. However, with any major decisions, I like to present the data and relay the impact of what any changes will have on the members and staff to Tim. He can make the final decision, but it's my responsibility to compile and present the data. I'm certainly not going to sit around in my office reading about how to do a proper glute bridge during my downtime. Instead, I leverage my time to analyze data and find improvements that will maximize net profit for the gym.

Savings vs. Revenue

Savings are just as important as revenue generation. Ultimately, both add to the bottom line, but revenue seems to get more attention in the fitness industry. Sales, sales, and more sales. More members, more members, and more members. Look, I totally get it. You must generate sales. You must grow and add members but finding areas where you can save is equally as important.

You'll see a little later on in this chapter how we increased our net revenue by saving on salary costs. Data helped me recognize an area we could optimize. For the director, finding areas to reduce costs is just as critical as being a great salesperson.

Analyzing the financial statements can be a great place to start, but also just being aware. Sometimes, employees don't pay as close attention as they should, because they're not writing the checks. Things like cable TV and towel service can go. Consider dividing up some cleaning duties and cutting back on your cleaning service frequency or buying supplies in bulk to get a discount. At the end of the year, it all matters on the balance sheet.

Finally, shop around and negotiate. There are plenty of vendors and most are willing to make a deal. Don't just accept a price -- hustle and pay as much attention to crunching pennies as you do to finding new revenue.

Now let's discuss some of the systems I use to be an effective director.

Tracking Leads & Managing Sales

It's extremely rare for me to find even 10 minutes to sit down and call past leads. Between members walking into my office, staff requiring my direction, creating content, creating training materials, programming, performing consultations, following up with active trials, compiling and analyzing data, etc., I have a hard time sitting down and prioritizing calling past leads. If a fresh lead comes in and I just happen to be sitting at my desk and see it, I'll hop on the phone and call. Usually though, by the time I see it, our front desk staff has beat me to it.

Because Tim Lyons is such a master at automation, when we have a new lead come in, it goes onto a shared Google sheet and directly into an automated nurture campaign in KEAP. The lead will start receiving automated text messages, voicemails, and emails, but we still reach out manually a minimum of three times. All the attempts or correspondence are documented on the Google sheet. So, when a new lead comes in, I can easily look and see who contacted them and what happened.

It's something I see, Tim sees, and the front desk sees. We all know what's going on and who did what. If something doesn't get done or there isn't follow through, it's quickly identified and corrected. The concept of a team is important here. If I have time, I call. If the front desk sees the lead first, they call. If it comes in on the weekend and nobody sees it, automation sends them a voicemail, text, and email, and then we call as soon as we get in on Monday.

It's the ultimate system for nurturing and tracking leads and for all those gym owners out there reading this, there is no way I could direct without the automation. Without this system, all my time would go to tracking, calling, and following up with leads. I would not be a director; I would be a salesperson with a glorified title. I wouldn't have time for the members or the team.

Remember how we discussed identifying needs and positions within your business? Either hire a full-time salesperson or for a fraction of the cost, have Tim set up automation for you and let your director direct!

Setting the Tone and Onboarding Members

Most of our members start on a paid 14-day trial, which means that they do a consultation, try it out for 14 days and then have to sit down with me again to convert. It's not the most efficient sales process, but in today's competitive market, it's a reality. Most of the time, people want to try us out before they commit for a year, which is totally understandable. Regardless of whether someone converts from the initial consultation or purchases a trial, the importance of setting the tone and onboarding them correctly cannot be overlooked.

I have a standardized worksheet that I use during consultations to take notes, highlight goals, FMS scores, and pretty much write down anything that's going to be important for my team in delivering the best experience possible for that individual. On the back of the worksheet, I have two boxes.

DIRECTING FITNESS

The first is a checklist of all the things that need to happen if someone signs up for a 14-day trial. The second, is a checklist of all the things that need to happen if someone signs up for a membership. I may finish a consultation and then have to dive right into another meeting or hop out on the training floor. The checklists are for me, to eliminate human error and make sure I don't forget anything. Consistency matters and if a step gets missed, it could mean the difference of thousands of dollars for the business and helping someone who really needs it.

Your checklist will look a little different in your business, but it's important to sit down and figure out exactly what steps should happen when you get a new trial and what happens when you get a new member. This is what mine looks like:

Kickstart Checklist

- [ ] Master Gym Form Checked "Converted to Kickstart" with Start Date
- [ ] Schedule All Training Sessions
- [ ] Coaches Card Created & Placed in Trials Folder
- [ ] Save Coaches Card in Dropbox
- [ ] Hand-Written Thank You Letter Sent

ZACHARY J. COLUMBIA

New Member Checklist

- ☐ Master Gym Form Checked "Converted to Membership" with Start Date
- ☐ New Member Photo Taken & Added to Mindbody Profile & Drop Box "Pulse Client Photos" Folder
- ☐ Member Given Key Fob & Shown How to Check-In
- ☐ Perkville Levels Board Explained
- ☐ Member Given Welcome Bag
- ☐ Myzone Belt Set Up
- ☐ Hand-Written Thank You Letter Sent
- ☐ Create Coaches Card & Client Folder – Save in Dropbox

Put yourself in the customer's shoes and map out the process. What do you feel would be important if you were them? What do you want them to learn about being a member? You only get one shot at onboarding someone, so make the most of it and don't forget anything. MAKE CHECKLISTS! Don't leave it up to chance; it's not worth the risk.

The "Standard"

"The Standard" and "The Standard Workout" are the newest additions to the lineup of Pulse systems. The idea came about during one of our weekly team meetings, while discussing the member experience. As a team, we created a list of 10 things every member should experience each time they frequent the gym and five things that make up a great workout. Here are the lists:

The Standard

- Leadership - control the member's experience
- Greet every member by name and with a smile
- Start and end on time
- The environment - music, cleanliness, aroma
- Recognition & Complementing
- Sense of Community
- Laugh
- Have a great workout
- Send off and thank you
- Accessibility to the staff

The Standard Workout

- Energy, Enthusiasm, Engagement
- The Workout Structure: Dynamic Warmup, Movement Prep, Primary Block, Secondary Block, Core & Isolation, Met Finisher

- Queuing: Visual, Verbal, Touch
- Coaching: Form, Tempo, Weight
- Personalize: Relate & Educate

The "Standard" isn't just a list of ideas, it's a list for me as director to manage off of. As a team, we put a lot of thought into what we felt was important to the member experience.

The member experience is directly tied to conversion of trials and retention of members. That's what the team came up with and agreed upon. It's our plan of execution. If we perform in these areas, conversions and retention should take care of themselves. As the director, these are my performance checklists to hold the staff accountable. If one of the team members doesn't perform in any of these areas and check the box so to speak, I can address it and depersonalize it. It removes any gray area, sets a clear expectation, helps the team understand how their individual performance directly impacts the business, and allows me to speak to their failures without it feeling like a personal attack.

Most of the items on our lists were already being performed most of the time, but not every time, and not in the same way. Not the Pulse way. We took these two lists, broke them down, elaborated on them, explained them, and then trained on them until they became second nature and inherently built in. We trained on them until they became our standard and continually revisit them. Remember, even championship caliber teams need regular practice!

Annual vs. Month-to-Month

One of the things I've gone back and forth on over the years is whether or not selling annual contracts pays off. There is actually a substantial divide in the fitness industry, where on one side, you have the mindset that an annual contract creates a barrier during the sales process. On the other side, many gym models believe that the annual contract increases retention and customer lifetime value. I see both sides as valid points and I believe both models have a place in your gym.

Before implementing anything in your gym, you should always ask yourself, "How does this affect my customers?" and "How will this be perceived by my customers?" You must put yourself in their shoes and look at each procedure and policy from every possible angle. Sure, as a business owner, I would want every single person to be locked into an annual contract, because I would know exactly how much money I was going to make over the next year. As a customer, I might be concerned about things like: trainers quitting, decline in service, moving, losing my job, etc.

What good is an annual contract anyway? If someone breaks it, what are you going to do, send them to collections? An annual contract is really a fiat contract. It's psychological and really only provides a commitment from the member as long as they're committed. Why would you create a barrier at the point of sale? Why not just advertise "No Contract" as a selling tool? The answer is simple. Results require commitment and accountability.

We know most people can't succeed on their own and won't stick with something long-term. You can and should use the annual contract as a selling tool for your benefit. Now if you meet with someone who loves to work out and is what I call a gym whore -- meaning they get bored easily and bounce from gym to gym -- you'll probably lose that person if you try to sell them an annual contract. You can offer it to them but be prepared to bribe them if you want any chance at closing them.

On the other hand, if you meet with a prospective client who has tried and failed, started and stopped, and binged and dieted, then they're your ideal candidate to sell an annual contract to. It's an easy pitch. "This time Mr./Mrs. Prospect, we're not going to let you fail! We're going to be invested in your success, but you have to meet us halfway. I need a commitment from you that you won't give up this time." Handshake, sign, done deal!

DIRECTING FITNESS

I'll be perfectly honest with you, it doesn't matter whether you sell annual contracts or month-to-month, both will create headaches for you. I can't tell you how many times I've had to deal with an angry member who requested to cancel the day before their monthly autopay hit and were furious when they still got billed the next day. Policies and procedures mean nothing to the client who feels as if you've been their best friend since they joined. The client coach relationship is really something. Try holding a member to an annual contract? It usually doesn't end well. Try standing your ground and most likely you'll be fighting it out with them over public internet reviews. What I've found works the best is to create a policy that seems like a win for the member, but also protects the business.

Protecting your business financially is obviously really important, but protecting your business's reputation is equally as important. Unfortunately, this is a constant balance struggle in the director role. However, it's imperative for the director to fight for the financial wellbeing of the business, while still ending every relationship on a positive note. Luckily, you have this book to point you in the right direction and I'm going to explain to you some best practices in handling different situations and conflicts.

Provide the simplest (and fairest) early termination policy ever! Offer both annual contracts and month-to-month.

Price the month-to-month higher. I like $100 more per month, but you can use whatever makes the most sense for your business. If someone is in an annual membership and wants to cancel early, just charge them the difference of what they would have paid as a month-to-month member. For instance, if someone pays $300 per month for an annual contract, then the month-to-month contract is $400 per month. Sell them the annual and explain that if they want to cancel early, they'll owe $100 for each month they were a member. So, if someone wants to cancel after three months, they owe $300 as an early termination fee. Unless someone plans on moving and doesn't want to pay out one lump sum at the end, you'll almost always be able to sell an annual agreement. Paying the difference seems to make more sense to the member and seems fairer from their point of view. I've never received a single complaint from a member when holding them to this, either.

With that being said, you will run into the prospect that refuses to sign a contract no matter what. I would never suggest turning those people away, even if you must give them the annual rate to close the deal. If I do this, I always charge an initial fee though to cover our cost of acquisition and welcome packet.

Membership Freezes

As I previously mentioned, freezes created a huge problem for us. Not only did it kill our recurring revenue during the summer months, but nearly 40% of members never came back. Another issue is that members would request to go on freeze a day before their monthly autopay was scheduled to come out. Even though our previous policy had required 14-day notice, not once did I ever have a member that didn't complain about still being billed. There are two simple strategies we implemented to deal with membership freezes.

Annual Contract Freeze: I made it very clear in the sales consultation that an annual membership meant we would bill and collect for 12 consecutive months. If the member wanted to go on freeze they could, but we would still collect the money and tack it onto the end of their membership period as prepaid.

Not only did this freeze policy help us make financial decisions as a business, but it also prevented members from freezing and never returning. Additionally, it helped protect our monthly EFT during slower months and spread the financial burden of freezes across the entire year.

Month-to-Month Freeze: Instead of requiring members to give us 14-day notice, we didn't require any notice. We let members go on freeze at any point but collected their next scheduled payment. That payment was then applied to their membership when they returned. Since members had already paid, they were much more likely to return. This also prevented them from turning their membership off and on simply because they didn't want to spend the money.

Scheduling

Scheduling. I love scheduling. Scheduling is my favorite... Okay, the reason I hate scheduling is because you can't please everyone, and I don't just mean the staff. Members will get used to working with a specific trainer or trainers and changes to the schedule might not thrill them. Finding the most efficient schedule is a balancing act between accommodating coaches, accommodating clients, and doing what's best for the business.

As director, I've had the coaches on normal shifts, two long shifts and three short shifts, rotating shifts, and even four-day work weeks. You name it, I've implemented it. The secret is really letting the data tell you what to do. It's important to utilize reporting and analyze trends in determining when you should offer training and how many coaches you need.

I'll give you an example. I did a complete attendance analysis to understand how many training sessions we needed available, what times were most profitable, and what times we could dump without hurting the business. What I found was that we could eliminate certain training times and direct members into slower times to fill up available training slots. I used this information to identify our staffing needs and develop a staff schedule. By shrinking availability and filling up what had been empty training slots, we not only increased our hourly net profit, but were also able to eliminate an entire coach's salary without negatively impacting members.

It wouldn't have been possible to optimize our schedule this way without understanding and leveraging the data. Sure, it's always nice to be able to accommodate coaches and please the clients, but data is really the key to creating as near a perfect schedule as possible. This is a schedule that minimizes costs and maximizes profit.

Don't Just Think It, Ink It

It's really important to keep a client notebook. I have one-off conversations with members all the time about some independent situation or circumstance I must manage outside of standard operating procedures. If I tell a member something and then three months later, they act on it... Well, I'm telling you right now, the odds of me remembering our conversation are not good. However, there's about a 150% chance of them remembering that at exactly 8:15:36am on Tuesday Dec 5, 2014 what I said word for word!

For instance, I had a member come to me and say they were going to be out of town for about half the month. Instead of offering them a discounted rate for the month, I suggested they make up their unused sessions when they got back. (Not a typical way of doing things, but we get the money this way and it's a solid compromise with a "challenging" member.) A couple months later when they went over their allotted monthly sessions and got charged an overage fee, they weren't too happy. Did I remember that I told them it was okay? Of course not. It might not really seem like a "system," but you need to write this stuff down! Trust me, keeping track of conversations is as much a system as the sales process.

I was only going to use that one example, but literally this morning another one popped up and I just had to share.

I pulled into the gym parking lot this morning and as I headed toward the door, I noticed a familiar looking face out of the corner of my eye. I heard a voice say, "Just the man I wanted to see." I turned and looked, and it was a past member I hadn't seen in over two years. Unfortunately, she had been diagnosed with breast cancer several years prior. I loved training her, because even after undergoing several rounds of treatment, she continued to come and workout. Eventually though, it became too much, and the doctors told her she had to stop. I have a great deal of respect for her. Anyway, we cruised into my office and caught up for a bit.

When it came time to sign her back up, she said, "Do you remember two years ago when I got charged for an extra month and instead of refunding me you said you would just credit it towards my membership when I started up again?" Gulp! I was thinking "No! How could I possibly remember that," but that's not what I said. Afterall, that sounds like something I would totally have done to keep the money and not have to issue a refund. (Always a good practice in my humble opinion.)

It's actually pretty comical that happened while I was working on this section of the book. Anyway, I like to use Microsoft Notepad, and save the documents in a folder on my desktop, but you can use anything that works for you. Trust me, it's worth taking 60 seconds to jot down something you told a member. You never know when you might need to revert back to it.

Bend Don't Break

This isn't exactly a system, but I think it's important to mention here. The biggest challenge any training gym faces is retention. I know of maybe two gyms that have a waiting list. Wouldn't that be nice?

I think because we face such a daunting challenge of retaining members, that we tend to compromise too much.

Any director or gym owner knows from experience that the second you try to stand your ground with a client over anything financial or anything regarding company policy, they're gone and are never coming back. So, when should you give in and when should you stand your ground?

Well first of all, let me say that this isn't just a dilemma that directors or gym owners face. It's a major problem among trainers too, though their issue is not around policy. It's not uncommon for trainers to allow their clients to get away with too much or do something they don't agree with.

I remember one time when I was performing a consultation with a couple who came in because they both wanted to lose weight. They explained that they had been doing one of those stupid, and quite frankly unhealthy, meal replacement shake programs for several months. It worked well for them at first, but they had stopped seeing results and decided they needed to add a training program in. Wanting to make the sale, I went along with it and signed them up, knowing they needed to stop doing their multi-level marketing shake if they ever wanted to see results from working out. What I should have done was not compromised. I should have explained everything to them right then and there. Why? Because they didn't get results and they didn't stick around!

I tell my coaches all the time, the minute you compromise and let your clients get away with something you know is wrong, that's the second you lose them. It may take a week or a month, or even a year, but they'll eventually quit because you didn't do what you knew was right all along. Sure, we need to be compassionate, but these people are coming to us for our help. We're the experts! Don't compromise when it comes to the client's results. Educate them and stand your ground. If you bend, you break.

Second, when it comes to policy and finances, it's not so black and white. Big box gyms don't build the same types of relationships with their members that training studios do. In big box gyms, the policy is the policy and that's the end of it. Stay. Leave. No one cares. Our business model doesn't usually have the luxury of being so brazen or indifferent.

Make good friends with your clients. Talk about their life, kids, spouse, job, vacations, etc. Have them bring you baked goodies and give you gifts and bonuses. Then, stand up for your company policies and tell them no. See what happens… They'll look at you like you stole their puppy or kicked their grandma's cane out from under her. I've seen clients go from being my best friend to instantly looking at me like I'm Satan. They'll leave you positive reviews and tell you how grateful they are for changing their life; and then bam, "Cancel my membership!" comes out of their mouth faster than Wyatt Earp could draw a six shooter. It's a challenge that's totally unique to our environment and how you handle it can mean the difference between keeping or losing a client.

    This is where I play the "bend don't break" card. Giving a little here is totally different than a client telling you they're going to eat pizza and drink beer on the weekends and still expect to get results. In my experience, if you stand strong on your policies, it'll lead to a cancellation. I'm not sure if it's even so much that the member is upset about the issue, as much as it is that they feel hurt because you wouldn't accommodate them. Regardless, compromising and keeping the member is always better than losing them, especially on bad terms.

    When a member comes to you upset or asking you to do something that's contrary to company policy, step one is to diffuse the situation. The best way I've found is simply to listen. Ask them to explain the situation to you. Pay close attention to anything that keys you into the underlying issue, which usually is unspoken. Not only does allowing the member to vent communicate that you're invested in helping them, but it also will help you gauge as to how far you need to bend in order to accommodate them. Sometimes by listening, I realize that if they don't get what they want they're gone, and sometimes they're asking for something so minimal, giving it to them has little or no impact on the business.

    In either of these cases, I make it seem like it's a huge deal for me to give them what they want. Hey, might as well earn some bonus points in their eyes while I'm at it. Then, I wait for them to walk out of my office happy. As soon as they get out the door, I get up from my desk and call them back in. I meet them at the entrance and say, "Hey since I did that for you, can you do something for me?" First, I ask them not to tell anyone what I did for them. That protects me and it makes the client feel even more special. Second, I ask them for anything I want at the time; like a positive review, a testimonial, or to model in a photo shoot for us. Whatever the need is at the time.

Remember how I mentioned the director role is like being a politician? This is a perfect example.

DISCLAIMER: It's bad business practice to treat members differently and you have to be extremely cautious about what individual accommodations you are willing to make. I always ask myself, what will happen if other members find out? If you'd be unwilling to accommodate every member in the same way, then you have to be willing to say "no."

There are also times when you must try to meet in the middle. In which case, after I hear them out, I always like to say something to the degree of, "I understand where you're coming from," and then explain the purpose for the policy we have in place.

As the director, I have the luxury of not being the final decision maker. This allows me to compromise a little and explain that it's outside of my ability to do any more than that for them. If you're a franchise owner, you can use the same tactic. If you're an independent gym owner, you're stuck trying to sell some empathy to the member.

Regardless, the best outcome is always the one that keeps the member. If possible, the director should find a work around. If it's not reasonably possible and the member is going to leave, the goal then becomes to salvage the relationship, end on good terms, and avoid a negative review.

DIRECTING FITNESS

Redefine and Reconnect

What improvements are needed for your current system?

"There exist limitless opportunities in every industry. Where there is an open mind, there will always be a frontier."

Charles F. Kettering

Chapter 8
The Medical Assistant Close

Relationship with Money

Before we talk about my approach to sales, I want to reiterate the point that great coaches know their value. This is such an important area that most gym owners and directors don't train on.

One of the most difficult things for coaches to do is "take" someone's money and be okay with it. Lack of money is an interesting and relatable topic to just about every fitness professional out there. Most trainer's live paycheck to paycheck. When someone tells them they can't afford it, they accept it, and immediately let them off the hook. They shake their hand, walk them to the door, and wish them all the best, as they watch them drive away in their BMW.

If you've ever done that as a personal trainer, raise your hand. Don't worry, we all have, and shame on us for it.

If someone tells us they can't afford our services and we accept it, we've prioritized money over health. Worse, it's not even our money! Real coaches don't do that!

We always try to explain to people that without health, they have nothing. Being healthy means being able to take care of their family, being more productive at work, feeling energized, and preventing health issues. As a fitness professional, it is an absolute requirement to get people to understand why investing in their health is so important and so foundational to every other aspect of their lives.

In order to have success in the fitness industry, having a healthy perspective and relationship with money is required. My #1 rule to sales is to never care about someone else's money. Now, that's only part of my #1, but I feel like it was important to separate in order for you to really grasp the point. I couldn't care less about how you spend your money. Why? It's not mine. If you want to go out and buy an expensive car, it doesn't matter to me. It doesn't affect me in the least. Never be invested in how your clients spend their money. It's none of your business.

Are you ready for the second part of my #1 rule to sales? Never care about someone else's money as much as you care about them.

Now remember, coaches know their value. I'm not saying you need to work for free just because you love your clients. That would be like the mom who doesn't have time to work out because she's too busy taking care of everyone else. What I am saying is you need to charge whatever it takes for you to help your clients and not ever worry about them being able to pay. Again, it's not your money they're spending and here is the real kicker; they need to spend the money, otherwise they won't do it!

There is a scripture in the Bible that says, "For where your treasure is, there your heart will be also." Now whether you are religious or not, you understand the point.

If you want to be a great director, and if you want success in this industry, then you need a healthy relationship with money. You must be comfortable asking for and taking someone else's money. If you have confidence in yourself, in your team, and in the service you're providing, then the "ask" shouldn't be difficult. Don't focus on the money they are giving you, instead focus on how you and your team are HELPING them. People can always tell the difference between someone who is being genuine and someone who is just trying to make a sale. Explain to them UPFRONT that you care about them and the money is the insurance policy THEY NEED, to guarantee that they'll keep coming back.

If you're a director who does sales, I'm probably not telling you something you don't already know; but does your team? Even if your team isn't doing sales consults, they still need this mindset. Understand that your team is constantly selling whether directly or indirectly. They shouldn't be focused on the members' money; they should be hyper-focused on helping the member and doing what's best for the member. When we sell based on the money, the price will always be too high. When we sell based on what's best for the member, most will pay, no matter the price.

If you feel even the slightest bit uncomfortable when it comes time in a consultation to ask for money, then it's an indication that you're not confident in your value offering. A lack of confidence during the sale, means you either lack confidence in the model to deliver for the prospect or you lack confidence in your team. Both are a reflection on the director as a leader. Think about that!

The Presale

The presale is everything leading up to the actual consultation. It occurs from the point of contact to the tour and is probably the most overlooked step in the sales process. I don't know of any other business that suffers as many no-shows as we do in the fitness industry. One, motivation is fleeting and two, gyms are intimidating. You could get together with the most experienced successful trainers in the industry and sit for hours compiling a list of all the barriers that prevent people from showing up and making a buying decision. You could also sit for hours figuring out ways to eliminate those barriers. I don't believe there's any magic bullet, although, I do have a few suggestions that have worked well for me.

    First and foremost, pick up the phone and have a quick conversation with the prospect. Find out a little about their goals and what they're looking for. Not only will you be more prepared for the consultation, but you'll also already have established some rapport, which can go a long way in both getting them to show up and sign up. This doesn't always have to be done by the director, either. The front desk staff can speak with the prospect too and relay the information they collect. The comfort of knowing that there is a friendly person excited to meet with them can be the differentiator in show rate.

    Second, appear organized and professional. Again, have a system in place. Confirm your appointments through text and/or email and provide them with a brief written overview or welcome video of what to expect.

Finally, the most important step aligns with what we have already discussed in several chapters of this book. Be enthusiastic. Look forward to the opportunity to help someone and have a new member. Let your culture shine through the phone.

I know, sometimes consultations happen later at night, after you've already worked all day; but if the prospect picks up on the vibe that you'd rather be somewhere else; they're gone. Enthusiasm and energy make all the difference in the entire sales process and aren't only vital for the one performing the consultation, but the entire staff the prospect will come into contact with as well.

Consultative Sales

Honestly? Honestly... I hate sales and it's not because I'm bad at it. To me there is nothing worse than selling someone into a subscription-based service knowing they're going to regret it. Have I done it? Yes of course. Have I regretted it? Yes of course!

I don't like hard closes. Experience tells me that anytime I've ever hard closed someone just to make a sale, it's never been worth the money. They don't come to the gym, they email me to cancel, they don't answer my phone calls, and I email them back. They get mad that we have a cancellation policy and a termination fee (that they clearly acknowledged when I sold them into the agreement), but when we charge them money, they leave negative feedback on the internet. We then offer to refund their money if they remove the review, they do, and we let them off the hook, make a couple hundred bucks. In the end, it just wasn't worth it!

Honestly? Honestly... I don't actually hate sales. I like sales and I love helping people. I like guiding people to make the right decision for their health. I like identifying problems and providing solutions for money. I like seeing someone light up when they realize we have the solution they've been searching for. All of that is sales, but it's not always how the process goes.

I have one consultation approach that I've been using successfully for years now. I call it the medical close. When you visit the doctor, you never walk through the front door of the office and immediately meet with the doc. What happens? You walk up to the receptionist to check-in for your appointment. The receptionist will then hand you paperwork to fill out. Once you fill out the paperwork, a medical assistant comes and gets you. The medical assistant does all the preliminary screenings. They weigh you, check your vitals, and ask you about why you're visiting. Then you wait for a few minutes in the exam room until the doctor finally comes in.

When the doctor finally does come in, the patient knows it's time to get down to business.

Sales is quite tricky in the fitness industry. Unfortunately, prospects come in sort of expecting a hard-nosed salesperson and their guard is already up. Anything you do that seems gimmicky or over the top comes off as disingenuous. We've been taught that people buy based off of emotion and so often the fitness consultation is structured around getting an emotional purchase. While there is absolutely nothing wrong with a little emotion, it needs to be mature emotion. We're not in it for short-term one-time purchases. The medical assistant close is the perfect way to build rapport, communicate value, present solutions, create a mature emotional response, and establish authority.

Authority is one of the missing keys to many fitness sales approaches. It's critical that the prospect subtly perceives that the director or salesperson is coming from a position of authority. Authority directly relays the message that the one conducting the consultation has a valuable level of expertise and the solution that the prospect needs. When this becomes evident to the prospect, it creates a mature emotional response. Not a response of, "I need this right now!" Rather a response of, "I need to act now!" and there is a clear difference.

DIRECTING FITNESS

If a consultation gets an "I need this right now" emotional response, the salesperson can pat themselves on the back as being good at theatrics. Though, the reality is, that person will probably have buyer's remorse and not last long. They'll have a poor lifetime value. The person that recognizes they need to act now, understands that what they're signing up for is a process and a lifestyle change. Regardless of whether you use my consultation structure or not, your goal should be to get this type of response from the prospect.

Here is my exact process for the consultation:

Leverage your front desk staff! When you have a consultation scheduled, your staff should already have been in contact with the prospect over the phone, text, and/or email. When that prospect walks through the front door of your facility, they should be greeted by name) by a smiling and prepared front desk staff member. A "nice to meet you in person" with a firm handshake goes a long way! The first impression is imperative and sets the tone!

After the initial intro is over, the front desk staff will hand the person a clipboard with a liability waiver and questionnaire. As they are instructed to have a seat, the front desk staff will politely ask if they can get the prospect some water. After the prospect fills out the paperwork, the staff will have the prospect perform an InBody analysis, and then drop off their paperwork and results to me before taking the prospect on a tour of the facility. While the tour is happening, I examine the questionnaire and InBody results to develop a game plan for the consultation. As the tour comes to an end, the front desk staff walks the prospect to the door of my office, where I greet them and ask them to have a seat in a big comfy chair.

If everything goes as planned, my role in the consultation process should only take 20 minutes. As soon as I close the deal, the new member gets turned back over to the front desk staff for a brief onboarding and membership setup.

Think about that from a director or gym owner perspective. How valuable is your time? If your team is well-trained and you use this systematic approach to your sales consultation, you can free up a great deal of your time and either perform way more consultations, or focus on other areas that need your attention.

Selling Viagra

Alright, you're probably wondering what actually takes place between myself and the prospect during the consultation. By the time I sit down with the prospective member, they should have seen our facility, met several staff members, learned about our training philosophy, classes, operating hours, etc. In other words, they know who we are, what we do, and how we do it. At this point, it's my job to demonstrate to them how everything they just learned is the solution to accomplish whatever it is that they want to accomplish.

Sometimes, that's easier said than done.

One of the biggest issues that we face in the fitness industry is "The Idea" of fitness. People desire to be fit but want the shortcut. What makes you think that someone who is overweight will care enough about getting into shape that they'll research your business, schedule a consultation, and commit to a training program that requires them to completely change their entire lifestyle? It's not gonna happen! Well, okay, it might happen like 1 out of 100 times, but you can't run a successful business off of that.

There are really only two types of prospects you'll run into.

The first is the "Tell You Everything" Prospect. This person is so easy to sell. They love the idea of fitness. They want to participate in every type of workout program known to man and you'll have no problem getting them scheduled or closing the deal after they respond to your ad. I have nothing against these people because they truly see the value in working out. Just be prepared to hear their whole entire life story before you ever meet them in person. Be patient and listen. If you pay attention to what it is that they are saying, they'll give you plenty of opportunity to present your packaging and pricing to them. Usually if the "Tell You Everything" Prospect is handled correctly, you can hold out a paper with your training options and pricing on it and they will sell themselves.

The second type of prospect you'll run into is a much harder sell. I like to call this person the "Viagra" Prospect. I want you to imagine, if you can, how the conversation would go between a doctor and a man who has erectile dysfunction. A man walks into the doctor's office and in comes the doctor to ask him his reason for visiting.

The man says, "Well...I just haven't been feeling right lately."

"No?" asks the doctor. "What seems to be the problem?"

The man says, "Um... I don't have as much energy as I used to."

The doctor replies, "Hmmm... okay. Well, you are getting older, you know."

The man says, "No! That's not it, doc."

The doctor inquires, "Well, what seems to be different? Why do you feel like you don't have as much energy?"

The man answers, "I'm not sure what it is. I work hard, but I've always done that. I'm just not sure. I think maybe my testosterone levels are down or something."

"Oh," says the doctor. "What makes you think that?"

The man responds, "I'm not really feeling as energetic as I used to. Like... um... well... I've noticed a drop in libido."

The doctor says, "Ah, I see. Are you having trouble with erectile dysfunction?"

"Yeah..." answers the man, unassured.

      This is how 90% of fitness consultations go. It's so hard to get the "Viagra" Prospect to admit to you why they're actually meeting with you. Imagine how hard it is for a man to admit to a doctor that he has erectile dysfunction. Now imagine how hard it is for someone to admit that they feel uncomfortable in their own skin and feel shame when they look in the mirror!

This person isn't going to openly come out and say it, but if you handle them correctly, you'll get the sale.

Always assume that prospect is not going to be a cheap date. You can't give them one glass of wine and expect them to tell you everything. Be ready to dig and pry and get extremely personal. When you get the real answer, be ready to go in for the kill… I mean close.

It's necessary to assume that 100% of your leads are "Viagra" leads. This person takes nanoseconds to talk themselves out of continuing down your pipeline. Once they hit your funnel, you need to instantly be on them like white on rice. Call them. Nurture them. Get them sold as soon as humanly possible. Get them to sit down in front of you before they talk themselves out of it.

Once you get the prospect on the phone or in front of you, you need to get to the underlying reason for why someone has come to see you. Again, there is a 90% chance they are a "Viagra" Prospect.

One difference between the "Viagra" Prospect and the "Tell You Everything" Prospect, is that with the "Viagra" Prospect, you have one shot to close them. That's it! One shot! You can't give the "Viagra" Prospect options. If you give them options, they get overwhelmed. They revert back to all the things they've tried and failed. They listen to the little voice in the back of their head saying, "You can't do it," or "It's not worth it," and THEY ARE GONE!

Never present options! Never present packages and pricing. Present solutions.

No man goes to the doctor with ED just to talk; they go in wanting to leave with a definitive solution to the problem. Sell one package, one price, one result, one solution. Don't let the prospect leave with any doubt about what action they need to take to achieve their desired result.

Redefine and Reconnect

What's your consultation process?

How can you improve it?

"Anyone can hold the helm when the sea is calm."

Publilius Syrus

Chapter 9

Success Stories Only

The Secret to the Selling Sauce

There's a final point I'd like to make about selling and I believe it's so important that I gave it its very own chapter. It doesn't just pertain to prospective members, but to your current members as well. Not having it or losing it is one of the underlying reasons gyms continue to lose members and end up closing their doors.

If you've ever done any type of sales training ever, then you know the number one reason people decide to make a purchase is emotion. While that couldn't be truer in our industry, there is a major missing component to selling, and without it, you actually can't be successful in this industry.

If I were to ask you how to create emotion, what would you say? Most sales professionals are taught to ask why. To find the underlying motivation or pain point(s) and then focus on those. This is certainly a solid approach and it's one that any seasoned sales pro will incorporate in their consultation. However, we're still missing the secret to the sauce. So, what is it already?

Passion. Passion is not only the most important component in the sales process, but it's also the most important in retaining your members.

Sure, you might be able to stir up some emotion with a prospective member who is unhappy with their weight and appearance, but does your desire and enthusiasm to help them shine through? Does your body language and excitement communicate to the prospect you love what you do?

I don't care how slick a salesperson is, in the fitness industry, passion is an absolute requirement.

Ask any hall of fame athlete what makes a great coach. I guarantee none will disagree with this statement: A great coach is as much or more invested in the achievement of their athlete, as they are themselves. That right there, ladies and gentlemen, is called passion. That attitude and that kind of buy-in is what's required if you want the gym of your dreams. It's you and it's every member of your team sharing that kind of passion towards your members' achievements.

I believe one reason gyms fail is because they either never truly had, or they've lost their passion. For every success story, you'll have at least nine failures. You fail seven out of ten times in the game of baseball and you're an all-star. That's because not only is hitting a baseball extremely difficult, but there are nine players on the field and only one of you. The odds are stacked against you and the odds for us are so much worse -- it's not even close.

Remember how we started this book? Mission Impossible right? It's easy to lose your passion when you see so much failure. It's easy to lose your passion when you have cancellation after cancellation coming across your desk. The moment it becomes noticeable and begins impacting the members, is the moment a gym begins its downward spiral.

That passion starts to go missing during the sales consultations and even though you ask all the right questions and follow all the right steps, you won't be able to stir the emotions of the prospect correctly. Passion isn't something you say, it's something you feel. If you don't feel it, the prospect won't either.

So how then do we keep it, or go out and find it and bring it back? We change our perception.

DIRECTING FITNESS

It's known in the game of baseball; you go three for 10 and you're an all-star. You go complete three out of 10 passes in football and you're not going to be playing football very long. You only hit three out of 10 jump shots and basketball isn't the sport for you. The definition of success is different depending on what game you're playing. In our game, this fun little game called the fitness industry, three for 10 may not be realistic. Maybe one for 10 makes you an all-star and just like any great athlete will tell you, the next play is the most important.

Forget the failures. Forget the cancellations. Forget the prospects that told you "no." Forget the client you invested all your time and energy into who didn't listen and hit the fast food joint on their way home from the gym. Just forget it.

Focus only on the success stories. Focus on the client who hit their goal. Focus on the client who got their confidence back. Focus on the client who survived a heart attack because they started doing your program. Even focus on a client who you know isn't following protocol but feels better and is enjoying their life more. Just focus on those things. Focus on the positives.

Don't let the failures bring you down… don't even let them slow you down. And no matter what, don't lose your passion.

Redefine and Reconnect

In what ways do you hold onto your failures in ways that only self-sabotage?

How can you better focus your energy?

"Success is not final, failure is not fatal: it is the courage to continue that counts."

Winston Churchill

Chapter 10

Redefining The Fitness Director

As I previously mentioned, the director and gym owner positions are closely aligned. The mindsets should be remarkably similar, and each should understand and respect where the other is coming from. Much like the client/coach relationship, the director/gym owner dynamic shares its own uniqueness. Having open communication and being comfortable speaking your mind is necessary if you want to continue moving forward. Tim and I have a great relationship that has developed over the years and I would like to conclude this book by touching on how you can have the same relationship and mutual respect in your business.

Just Handle It

When the opportunity opened up at Pulse for director, another coach and I were competing to earn the role. I noticed that the other coach would constantly run into Tim's office to "ask" questions about how to do something or what should be done. I put "ask" in quotations because it was obvious to me that this individual's motive was really just to draw attention. I figured it was obvious to Tim too, so I decided to take the opposite approach. I would often ask myself, "If I were the owner, would I want to be bothered with this?" Most of the time, the answer was "No." I knew Tim was busy. He had an entire other company to run and me running into his office every few minutes to ask him unnecessary questions wasn't what he was looking for from the next director.

When things came up, when I needed to decide, most of the time I just handled it. If you ask any business owner, they'll tell you, they appreciate someone who can think critically, problem solve, and is willing to take action. As director, it's important to be able to make a decision and go with it. If you're really stumped or the impact on the business could be too great, that's when you need to ask for guidance. We all know how the situation ended up working out and who ultimately got the job.

The point is, if you're the director, or any employee in any business for that matter, use common sense and then be proactive. Trust me, in a busy environment, it's an admirable quality.

Speak Up

The director shouldn't just tell the gym owner what they want to hear. Sure, how you present things and bring up issues is incredibly important to creating constructive, solution-driven conversation, but if you want to be the leader and steer the ship, you have to speak up. Understand that you're in the position for a reason, and that the owner is relying on you to be the voice of the team and the voice of the clients. Look at it this way -- you can either be a respected leader or a robot. Which do you think is more valuable and near irreplaceable?

Gym owners, it should go without saying, but listen and respect the director's opinions. If you disagree, cool, you're the boss. Use the opportunity as a learning experience, but don't discourage feedback or you won't ever get it again. Understand that from the director's point of view, they are trying to balance managing the team, taking care of the existing members, driving sales, and being a good steward of your investment. It can be challenging and if you feel like an area is lacking, sometimes all that's needed is offering support and communicating your trust in them to get the job done.

Business Is Business

In Chapter 3, I explained how emotional maturity for the director is paramount. One of the interesting things about emotional maturity is that it requires eliminating emotion. Not really, that would be humanly impossible; but instead, it's about controlling your emotions and not letting them get the best of you. Because the gym owner and director work so closely together, it's critical to separate emotion from business. Nothing is personal and keeping this in the forefront of your minds gives both parties clearer insight into finding solutions to problems and continuously improving.

Of course, I've screwed up and made mistakes. I'm human and there is always a learning curve in this business. Gym owners make mistakes all the time. I'm sure if you asked, they could easily think of 10 situations they wish they had handled differently. If you're doing your job as a director, being proactive, and making executive decisions, expect to make mistakes and be reprimanded for it. It's not a personal attack. You're not losing your job. Just learn from it and don't make the same mistake again.

Loyalty

Loyalty seems to be growing less common these days. It's not unusual for people to jump from company to company in order to climb the corporate ladder as opposed to starting at the bottom, working their way up, and retiring after 30 years with the same company. This couldn't be truer than in the fitness industry. I don't know of a single person who has spent their entire career with one gym. It's really pretty sad, but I believe going all in goes such a long way in this business. It's up to the director to show that they are invested in the long-term success of the business, before they can expect it to be reciprocated from the owner. Sorry kids, but that's the way it is.

Gym owners have invested and risked too much to just openly trust, and odds are, they've been burned in the past by the "upstanding" character our industry draws. As a new director, do everything you can to demonstrate to the owner you're all in and just as invested in the success of the business as they are. Work 12-or 13-hour days, stay late for that extra consultation, come in early and cover for the staff member that's out, repair equipment, and scrub the toilets. Keep your head down, work your tail off, and eventually you'll earn the gym owner's trust and respect.

Gym owners, you play as important of a role in earning the loyalty of the director. It's essential to understand that if you find a director who is willing to put in the kind of work I just described and can act on the lessons of this book, it's going to be hard to keep them long-term. Someone who can effectively lead and direct a business with this type of work ethic, is a highly valued commodity. In order to keep them, they need to be compensated fairly, rewarded, and provided with the same benefits they can get from a competitor. As owner, it's imperative that you take the same approach to rewarding and engaging your director as the director does the rest of the team. If you don't want to lose them, put yourself in their shoes and understand their perspective. It shouldn't be hard to do, because you probably spent quite a bit of time in their role... and what happened? You progressed, you grew, and you moved on to bigger and better things. Think about the value this individual brings to your team and what an asset they are to have. Reward their loyalty with your loyalty.

Redefining The Fitness Director

The building and equipment might be the most expensive asset in the business, but a great team is the most valuable. I'm going to go out on a limb right now and say that there will never be a successful gym that offers robot personal trainers. No matter how advanced technology gets, this business requires a personal, human touch. You cannot put a price tag on a director who can bring a bunch of individuals together, coach them, get them to perform at a high level, and unify them.

Does the gym owner: Have the expertise to do this? Have the time to do this? Want to do this? Is it a misallocation of resources? Would their time be better spent elsewhere? Are they spending their time working IN the business instead of ON the business? What are their long-term goals anyway? Do they want to be in the gym interacting with clients and addressing their problems every single day, or would they rather manage as a private investor manages their portfolio through a broker?

All these are necessary questions that get the gym owner to recognize what it is they want from their business and what it is they need out of the director position.

I think of Tim as my client. He's the investor and I'm his money manager. I'm looking out for his best interests and working to maximize his return on investment. Just like a stockbroker, I study the business! I examine the data. I keep up with industry trends. It's my responsibility as a steward of someone's investment to understand what their financial goals are. It's important for me to provide full transparency and it's necessary for me to understand the risks associated with each move I make with someone else's money.

Directors out there need to understand the faith that's being placed in them and the grave responsibility of their role. You are the manager of someone's investment. It is your obligation to grow that investment. This is the real definition of a fitness director.

Talk about #relationshipgoals for the gym owner and director! As an owner, imagine the lifestyle this type of relationship with your business would give you. For the director, imagine the prestige, pride, and -- of course -- financial reward you'll have from approaching your position this way.

Redefine and Reconnect

How can you better your relationship with those under you?

_____
_____
_____
_____
_____
_____
_____

How can you hold yourself accountable for your mistakes, without letting those mistakes get you down?

_____
_____
_____
_____
_____
_____
_____

"There are two ways of spreading light: to be the candle or the mirror that reflects it."

Edith Wharton

ZACHARY J. COLUMBIA

Directing Fitness Coaching Program

Thank you for reading Directing Fitness. The lessons detailed in this book are a great place to start.

To learn more about continuing development and the Directing Fitness Coaching Program, check out:

www.DirectingFitness.com

www.ingramcontent.com/pod-product-compliance
Lightning Source LLC
Chambersburg PA
CBHW052355220526
45465CB00003BA/1116